SEXUALITY AND AGING

Revised

Edited by Robert L. Solnick

12/2/82

This Monograph is published by the
Ethel Percy Andrus Gerontology Center
University of Southern California

RICHARD H. DAVIS, Ph.D.
Director of Publications and Media Projects

Editorial Assistant: Jean Rarig

© 1978 THE ETHEL PERCY ANDRUS GERONTOLOGY CENTER
First Printing 1978
Second Printing 1980

THE UNIVERSITY OF SOUTHERN CALIFORNIA PRESS

ISBN 0-88474-044-7

Library of Congress Catalog Card Number 78-51932

Book Design: Richard Bohen

Contents

IMPLICATIONS FOR NURSING CARE

THE ROLE OF LOVE IN LATE-LIFE SEX

Preface

Emphasis on the sexual needs and behavior of the older adult has increased remarkably since publication of the first edition of *Sexuality and Aging* in 1975. Since that time there has been a proliferation of newspaper, magazine, and journal articles as well as entire books on the subject of sex in the later years of life. However, there remain areas relating to sex and the older adult that are not being dealt with as part of the overall subject matter. In this second edition of *Sexuality and Aging* we have expanded our efforts to compile in one sourcebook viewpoints on sexuality which are not available elsewhere. In keeping with the Ethel Percy Andrus Gerontology Center's multidisciplinary perspective, contributors to this book include biologists, medical doctors, social psychologists, psychologists, sociologists, nurses, social workers, and program administrators.

The chapters have been grouped under five headings. The first major topic focuses on background information and attempts to sensitize the reader to the nature of the problem. In many ways the two chapters under this heading reflect a strong sociological flavor.

Next, the physiological, psychological, and sociological issues related to sexuality in the later years are examined. Sexual behavior patterns, physiological changes, psychological responses to changes, and the role of medical problems are considered in the next four chapters. The reader may feel that the Rossman chapter sounds a note of pessimism in an otherwise optimistic ambience; however, only if one is performance-oriented rather than pleasure-oriented does this become the case. Certainly Dr. Rossman, as well as the other contributors, encourages older adults to realize their full potential no matter what they may be. For most persons the potential is far beyond their current level of functioning.

Sexual growth, the third section of the book, is the subject of three chapters which deal with the resolution of specific sexual problems as well as with means for enhancing sexual pleasure when no specific dysfunction can be identified. The chapter by Monea presents personal growth techniques and some teaching techniques.

The impact of changing sexuality with age on the helping professions (particularly those involved in nursing care) is the fourth point of focus; three chapters are devoted to this important subject. The plight of the nursing home resident, still a neglected area of inquiry, receives increased emphasis in this second edition.

The fifth and final topic of the book discusses love and its relationship to sex and aging, an area totally new in this second edition. The changing role of love as persons move into their later years is treated in a sensitive and illuminating manner in the two chapters making up this important section.

Contributors to this volume represent diverse locations and significant activities. Dr. Carlfred Broderick, Professor of Sociology at the University of Southern California, also serves as Consultant on Sexuality to the American Medical Association. Dr. Robert N. Butler has recently become Director of the National Institute of Aging in Bethesda, Maryland. Bonnie Genevay acts as Consultant in Aging, Family, and Child Service of Metropolitan Seattle as well as Trainer in Sexuality and Aging.

Myrna I. Lewis is a social worker in private psychotherapy practice in Washington, D.C. Dr. Martin P. Loeb serves as Professor of Social Work and Director of the Faye McBeath Institute on Aging and Adult Life at the University of Wisconsin-Madison. Dulcy B. Miller functions as Administrative Director of the White Plains Center for Nursing Care. Helen Elena Monea is working as a private gerontology lecturer and author in the San Francisco area. Dr. Eric Pfeiffer, recently at Duke University, North Carolina, is now Professor of Psychiatry at the University of Colorado School of Medicine in Denver.

Dr. Margaret Neiswender Reedy is a Senior Staff Associate at the Andrus Gerontology Center, University of Southern California, Los Angeles. Dr. Isadore Rossman serves as Medical Director of the Home Care and Extended Services Department of Montefiore Hospital and Medical Center, Bronx, New York. Dr. Alexander Runciman is associated with a private clinic in Sherman Oaks, California, and holds a faculty post at the California State University at Northridge. Dr. Robert L. Solnick, senior editor of this work, is a member of the La Paz Psychological Group in Mission Viejo, California, and engaged in teaching and lecturing in the field of gerontology.

Professor Bernita M. Steffl is a member of the faculty of the College of Nursing, Arizona State University, Tempe. Dr. Mary Ann P. Sviland, a clinical psychologist in private practice in Canoga Park, California, also serves as a lecturer in the Psychology Department of California State University at Northridge. Mona Wasow is Clinical Assistant Professor of Social Work, University of Wisconsin at Madison. Dr. Ruth B. Weg is a member of the faculty of the Leonard Davis School of Gerontology of the University of Southern California, Los Angeles.

Although this book may not be a complete compilation of the subject matter on sexuality and the older adult, it does bring together various aspects of the topic. It should be valuable as a primary or a supplementary text for various types of classes, depending on the group's focus. The editor also forsees its usefulness in conjunction with special workshops.

It is a great pleasure to acknowledge the complete cooperation of the authors and their publishers in granting permission to include material which first appeared elsewhere. Also, a special thanks is due to Jean Rarig, whose efforts and talents guided the book through its lengthy and arduous development.

Robert L. Solnick, Ph.D.
January, 1978

Sexuality and Aging: An Overview

Carlfred Broderick

Let us start with the beginning of life and those elements of sexuality that are introduced and learned early; then we can look at the implications of these elements for the end of life. Three different aspects of early sexuality can usually be distinguished. There are probably many more, but I want to mention no more than that. The first one is the basic fundamental identity of male or female which is taught very thoroughly and early. As you perhaps know, one child in a thousand is born with ambiguous, not fully differentiated sex organs. They are more like that of a three-month old fetus. Somehow in the last months of fetal development the sex organs don't develop the clarity and differentiation of structure that we associate with the different sexes. When those children are born, someone has to make a decision whether to give them a boy's name or a girl's name, thus conferring a masculine or feminine pronoun. This decision has long-term implications since the world functions on the basis of a dichotomy in the area of sex; there are only two bathroom designations—"Ladies" and "Gentlemen." It is by assignment, then, that we learn whether we are male or female.

It has been discovered that if a child had been assigned to the male sex and over a period of months or years the doctor determined that there was very little chance that the child would ever develop sex organs that would let him comfortably dress in boys' gyms or even to function comfortably, this person could be made surgically into an acceptable appearing female. In this case the doctor might convince the parent of the child that a sex change might be in the child's best interest.

You may be interested in the age at which you can make that sex change without risking psychological difficulties in the child; that is, how young should a child be for the sex change to be accomplished without trauma? The age is somewhere between two and three years of age. After that a change in the child's sex is very upsetting. By the age of three children know whether they are male or female. I think it is hard to fully appreciate how fully and how early we are taught that which as adults we take for granted.

The second element of sexuality is the learning of the social determinants of masculine and feminine behavior. Just what is masculine behavior, the masculine look, the masculine mannerism? And what are the feminine ones? In the French Quarter of New Orleans there are a great many bars where entertainment runs heavily toward sexual subjects of various kinds. Every other place features a female impersonator. It is interesting to observe that if you have a real live nude female on a swing, or lying on the bar, she just lies there; she has no need to do anything feminine; she is it. But if you see a female impersonator, he is working and strutting and wiggling, trying hard to capture the quintessence of femaleness. The performance is almost a caricature of femininity. The impersonators provide a better show than the naked girl by a large margin.

People get caught in changes in our society about what is feminine and what is masculine. A study done with college students in the late forties and redone in the late sixties shows that the average male today would place in the top one-sixth of the feminine end of that M-F scale designed in the forties. This doesn't mean that men are becoming more effeminate; instead, it means our concept of what is masculine has shifted so that not only long hair but also emotional warmth, interest in the arts, and being people-oriented have become accepted masculine characteristics. The average college male today is in the top one-sixth of what would have been a feminine direction twenty years ago. Thirty years ago you would find Marines or truck drivers as symbols of traditional masculinity. Interestingly, the 1968 study indicated that concepts of feminine behavior were unchanged. However, I am sure there has been a lot of change since 1968 through the Women's Liberation Movement.

What is masculine and what is feminine? Since the answer is socially determined, it can change, does change, and is changing. There is always a current set of rules about what is masculine and what is feminine. We always put people who are not near the mean of their own sex in a category that is not very socially approved. If I had a high squeaky voice, and my hips were too broad, and if I had gestures and mannerisms that you felt were inappropriate for a male, there is not one of you so professional that you would not raise a question. When we were children we had a certain sign which meant homosexual. It was very imprecise, but what we were responding to was deviations from the standard masculine or feminine norms as we knew them. We permit some deviation, but when people get beyond the permitted degree they are labeled and responded to as being deviant.

Finally, we must touch on heterosexuality and homosexuality, which differ still from behaviors discussed above. We now know that, aside from that subset of homosexuals who are anxious to thrust their homosexuality upon you (perhaps 20%), 80% of homosexuals cannot be distinguished by their walk, talk, or mannerisms from heterosexuals. In fact, even panels of psychologists who were sure they could distinguish categories found, when given what was in effect a lineup of homosexuals and heterosexuals, that they were wrong as often as they were right. We know that homosexuality and heterosexuality are separate phenomena from masculinity and femininity, having to do with whether you "turn on" to someone else's masculinity or femininity. That too seems to be learned behavior, though we don't know very much about it yet. We have more negative than positive evidence. More theories have been destroyed than have been supported, so right now we are more clear about what *doesn't* cause homosexuality than what does cause it.

We are not much more clear about what causes heterosexuality. Somehow all of us are born with the full capacity to "turn on" to anyone. Nevertheless, we find that through stages young people fantasize and rehearse what it would be like to be a member of the opposite sex—not necessarily genitally, but socially. By the time they reach full maturity they have long ago solved their male/femaleness; they have long ago established their style of masculinity or femininity. One of the qualities of the so-called "generation gap" is that people are living together in families who socialize on the basis of different standards of masculinity and femininity. We have established styles in our fantasies and behavior (heterosexually and homosexually) of our own sexuality. Those we carry through our adult life provide us with a great deal of our sense of identity as "I am a man," "I am a woman," and "I relate to people differently." I have noticed that the most outspoken women for the liberation movement have not found it useful or necessary to attack feminine style. Some of the most attractive women I know are women who make it very, very clear that they are not taking any gaff from any male. In order to do so they don't have to imitate my mannerism or my dress; stylistic difference is not even in jeopardy.

There are some important things happening in the three areas discussed above: for example, take male and female. Although male/female is learned, it is really not determined by what is between your legs. Still, genitals become a very important symbol of that. One of the things doctors have to cope with in performing a hysterectomy is the woman who comes out and says, "I am no longer a woman." That is, of course, foolish—but for her a uterus is the symbol of her self. If her self as a female resides in a uterus as a symbol and she loses the uterus, she may have a difficult time deciding where her new symbol of her self lies and whether it is female. That can happen to a young, middle-aged or older woman. It is interesting that one of the elements that has been least well dealt with in hysterectomies is the loss of a symbol of femininity itself. A mastectomy is a similar issue: what is it to be a woman without a breast, without a nipple? I have talked to women who have had mastectomies and who have long passed the desire to be nursing mothers, but as a symbol of themselves, as a symbol of their femininity and of their own self as a female, the breast had a significance to them that they felt strongly. There are differences in approach to these losses; these are challenges for many women as they are growing older.

It is relatively rare for the male to be castrated, to lose the obvious symbols of his masculinity. There are two very powerful exceptions which are less obvious: the first is impotence. I see many people in their forties, fifties, sixties, and seventies who have become very tense about their abilities to function sexually. There is nothing more recalcitrant than a recalcitrant penis. If you are trying to get it to perform, it seems that the harder you try, the more difficult it is. A man can suddenly feel incompetent. The very words "potent" and "impotent" unnecessarily generalize one's whole life. It's difficult, unless you have either been there yourself or have been very close to someone who has been there, to realize how important is the ability to function sexually if called upon to do so and how devastating is the inability to perform on cue. Men may say that their wives said it didn't matter, but eventually it did matter. Eventually the wife said, "Go and see a doctor." Eventually she said, "It is no fun for me either." Eventually she responded to him as though he were in fact impotent.

I think the other symbol of loss of masculine status is retirement. Perhaps the young people today feel that less of their identity as a male is in a job and the ability to earn money, but this is not true for most men over forty! Retired men, in addition to the problem of what to do with their time, are concerned with what symbols they are going to have of their own masculine identity to take the place of their lost job. I think we are not very good at helping men find these symbols, because just finding a hobby to fill their time isn't going to be enough.

Both men and women want their own sexual personal identity. Personal identity, at least from age two onward, has been compounded and interwoven and mixed with sexual identity. When you take somebody out of sex roles or make them so they don't function sexually to some degree, you attack not only their body but their image of themselves. When we are talking about sexuality in aging, I hope we are talking first of all about masculinity and femininity and how you keep a sense of being masculine and feminine. I have seen women of seventy and older in deep depression, almost a catatonic depression that nobody could seem to get them out of, until somebody thought of taking them to a beauty parlor. This experience was somehow reassertive of themselves as people of value, somebody worth responding to as a human being, as a female. I remember visiting a nursing home where a woman had an asthma attack. The doctor came in and drew her robe aside so he could get at her chest. She was in a convulsion of coughing; despite that, with one trembling hand she reached down and pulled her robe over her genitals. To me that was very human; what she was saying was, "I am still a woman." She wanted privacy, modesty. She was saying. "I am not just a symptom for the doctor." The privacy of a person is important, which is not too often recognized in nursing homes where the symbols of sexual modesty, personhood, privacy are so often ignored because they are just old people.

Another aspect of heterosexuality and homosexuality is the affectional aspect; that is, the aspect of sex as a mode of relating to other people. You don't have to be in bed to relate to people in ways that have to do with heterosexuality and homosexuality. It clearly matters in most cases that the person you are talking with is of the opposite sex. We grow from infancy being stroked, gentled, reaching out and kissing and holding and hugging as a way of expressing ourselves. But then in old age we are isolated – except when somebody comes with a needle or a napkin to clean up. I have never known anyone so old that they were not responsive to the warmth of a caress, to the holding, to the touching, and to the strokes that are associated with sex. It makes a difference to an old man whether the person who cares for him is a man or a woman; that's sex.

There are a lot of myths about sexuality in older people. In 1967 Isadore Rubin's book *Sexual Life After Sixty* came out and I was at that time doing a clinical internship in a Veterans Administration hospital. We had a staff conference every Tuesday morning: "staff seminar for enrichment." We didn't have that much to do, and we started taking turns reviewing books for each other that we had read. I picked up this one. We had a lot of older men in the VA, and I had the feeling that the staff wasn't very much in touch with their sexual needs. When I reviewed that book, it took me fifteen minutes to get that group of social workers, psychiatrists, psychologists, all people helpers, to calm down and get off the wise crack comments before they could be serious. They never fully achieved seriousness, because for them the concept of sex after sixty was a joke. They were surprised to find out that the age at which half of the men were still functioning sexually was seventy. We know that a large part of sexual functioning in the male, (especially the male, because the penis is so sensitive to beliefs and feelings), is psychological, is belief. How many of that other half of those 70 year olds could be sexually functional if they believed in it is an open question. My first thought was, how terrible it was that these people were working with older men. Then I had a second thought. I felt sorry, not only for the men who were being administered to psychologically by those other men who had such negative attitudes toward sexuality, but for the men and women themselves. If those were their beliefs about sexuality, then they were mocking their own sexual needs. They were making it indecent to have sexual needs and drives. Yet, when do we learn that people value you when they respond to you? When do we learn that one of the great rewards in life is to have someone touching and telling you nice things and how wonderful you are and responding to you as if you were a special and powerful person in bed?

I think that as we work with older people, I am hopeful that we will do so in the context not only of permitting older people who are married to have beds in the same room, but also in terms of not making fun of older men and women who want to live together even though they are not married. I am hopeful that we will think about socializing the people who are now younger and middle-aged to review their own views of sexuality and not to include in these views the withdrawal of sexuality as an expectation, the withdrawal of potency as an expectation. Hopefully, then, the man who comes home drunk one night and has an erection failure doesn't think he is over the hill, and "That's the end." He may never again be able to function because he told himself "This is what old age is like."

I am hopeful that, as we look at older people and their sexuality, our primary concern will be not only to treat them with dignity but also to permit them to be sexually attractive, to function as well as their circumstances will permit, and to encourage circumstances that do make it possible. More broadly, I hope that we can make inputs into both the rising generation and the aging generation so that they can feel their own humanness, and their own sexuality as part of their own humanness.

Reference

Rubin, Isadore. *Sexual life after sixty.* New York: New American Library, 1967.

Age Kills Us Softly When We Deny Our Sexual Identity 2

Bonnie Genevay

Dr. Mary Calderone (1971) ever reminds us that the spark of a new and zestful relationship can literally bring a sense of renewal of life itself to two older people previously convinced that life was forever finished. Yet—the woman or man inside the aging body often "dies softly" long before she/he is physiologically dead. When opportunity for us to function as sexual beings is denied us at the end of life, we have no way to deal with those timeless and ageless feelings—the deep need for expression of intimacy and affection—that are present until death. Irene Long (1976) pinpoints sex as an energy source:

> The truly sad thing about the strategic withdrawal of sex (in older people) is that sexual expression includes humor, teasing, twinkling eyes, better posture, conversational nuances and a general emotional lift. These add zest to life at a time when it is greatly needed.

9

Agism and Sexism

Dr. Nathaniel Wagner of the University of Washington has put his finger on it when he said, "It's OK for Strom Thurmond and Pierre Trudeau to marry women in their twenties, but if Golda Meir married a twenty-two year old male—even if he were Jewish—it would not be considered right!" (Rockey, 1976, p.4) Even with opportunities for partners, we who are older women too often subscribe to the insidious cultural injunction that we are not equal in attractiveness, sexual potential, and womanliness to younger women or to the "sexiness" (whatever that is) of aging male peers. This combination of agism plus sexism is a deadly deterrent to the full expression of humanness. It victimizes women at younger ages more than it does men in our society. It affects men heavily when their status as workers is also threatened—at the peak, or on the declining slope, of careers.

When racism is added to agism and sexism, we begin to glimpse the walls which close in upon minority women. As one very vivacious and beautiful black woman of seventy remarked, "They haven't seen me for a long time because I was black and a woman, and now they see me even less because I'm old!"

The first time I read Susan Sontag's (1972) searing and devastating description of "the visceral horror felt at aging female flesh" chills ran up and down my aging female spine:

> ...The point of women dressing up, applying make-up, dyeing their hair, etc., is not just to be attractive. They are ways of defending themselves against a profound level of disapproval directed toward women, a disapproval that can take the form of aversion... Aging is a process of becoming obscene sexually, for the flabby bosom, wrinkled neck, spotted hands, thinning hair, waistless torso, and veined legs of an old woman are felt to be obscene.

Lest we think that sexism and agism are modern inventions, hear this poem adapted by Louis Untermeyer from an ancient Greek anthology entitled *Ageless* (Rainer & Rainer, 1965, p.203):

Now Charito is sixty. But her hair
Is dark; her ample bosoms firm and fair;
Her skin is like a young girl's, warm and white;
Her legs and thighs are fashioned to delight.

Her years are in her favor, for she knows
Tricks that a novice never could disclose.
Yes, she is sixty; but, still full of fire,
She'll do, my friend, whatever you desire.

Embodied in this poem are agist and sexist stereotypes which you and I still unmindfully foster:

Poem	Agist Attitude	Stereotypical Response
Hair is dark, skin like a young girl's	It's OK to be chronologically old *if* you look young	"My dear Charito, you look so *young* for your age!"
Bosoms firm; legs and thighs delight	It's OK to be sexual at 60 *if* your flabby breasts & swollen legs don't remind your partner that aging and dying are realities	"*They* got married? I hope it works out (laughter). They're both on their last legs!"

If you feel I'm dwelling overlong on a centuries-old poem, consider this current and familiar agist ad which reflects our American youth-and-beauty cult and female competition value system:

> Now and then you like to be a step ahead of your friends. Now you can .. look younger than many friends your age. . . It's not a moment too soon to begin looking younger than friends your age! Use .. .. ..

And what if you do look older—considerably older—than friends your age? Are you no longer a valuable person, a sexual being? What this agist, sexist, skin-deep definition adds up to in an institutional setting at the end of life is competition between some women for the few men still available. Or the denial of sexual feelings on the part of women who practice the "if you don't compete you can't lose" non-sexual stance. Looking at men and women as sexual objects through "dating game" binoculars is circumscribing in youth; in old age it is dehumanizing and castrating of human affection and relationship.

Part of the tragedy—when we who are women buy into the stereotype that to be old is to be ugly and worthless—is the damage we do to relationships. In devaluing ourselves, the very men—husbands, lovers, sons, friends—whom we love and seek acceptance from are deeply affected. In counseling we are encountering increasing numbers of middle-aged and older men who find it impossible to buoy the flagging self and body images of the significant women in their lives. As the geriatric population grows, so do marital and couple communication problems—particularly after retirement brings partners together 24 hours a day.

A University of Washington study by Lenora Mundt (1975) examined how male and female clinicians (Broverman, Broverman, Clarkson, Rosenkrantz, & Vogel, 1970) defined "healthy" women as: more submissive, less independent, less adventurous, more easily influenced, less aggressive, less competitive, more excitable, more easily hurt, more emotional, more conceited about their appearance and less objective than men. Some of the older-old generation of women who have never had the opportunity for assertiveness training may fit some of these adjectives. This distorted view which clinicians hold of elderly women in particular may go unchallenged by them. Furthermore it is borne out by self-interpretations of Rorschach tests cited by de Beauvoir (1972). There is a great deal we who work with older women can do to confirm their strength, intelligence, beauty and power, and to disconfirm their agist and sexist definitions of themselves.

Some older people have swallowed the societal injunction that they are "bad" if they continue to be sexually expressive after their reproductive years are over. This oppression means hiding one part of ourselves from the rest of us, and it is an attitude applied to women, particularly from the middle years on. It is debilitating enough when we accept this attitude toward our sexual behaviors, but when we adopt this negativism toward our sexual desires, fantasies and feelings—with attendant guilt—we rob ourselves of life energy crucial to our existence! This particular tunnel-vision is non-chronological; it begins at 20 or 40 or 60—whenever our accumulation of losses (physiological, psychological, spiritual) affect our sense of worth, attractiveness and desirability.

Some older people try to talk to their doctors and other helping persons about being sexually active. They often encounter a shift in focus of their questions, selective responses, failure to deal with the sexual content of their concerns, or other evasions too subtle to confront. It is absolutely essential that all of us recognize that professionals are often ignorant of their agist attitudes and behaviors, and find it just as difficult as we do to imagine their elderly parents as sexual beings with unmet needs and desires. It is important that we who are clients and patients educate them—whether they want to be aware of their own aging sexuality or not!

And what of men who also experience our culture's sexist and agist definitions of what their looks, sexual performance, and socially acceptable mating behaviors should be? A very handsome (by any standards) but lonely 65 year old man shared his deep feelings. Listen for the "I'm too old" and "I'm not good enough" themes.

> I'm still caught in waves of passion at times. The only problem is I'm not lucky enough to have a partner any more. My wife died last year. It's too late for me to begin a third permanent relationship. The complications, the possible disappointment, of reaching out again are too much!

> I've been lucky with my health; only a little arthritis, high cholesterol, hypertension. But there are too many fears bound up with my sexuality now. I tried to have a relationship with a forty-year-old woman, but I couldn't get an erection. Sex is linked too much with being physically attractive. I'm still interested, but fear impotency.

> Fleeting intercourse with one person and another is just a form of high-class masturbation. One-night stands lose their meaning. I don't want a superficial relationship with another human being—I'd rather live alone. But it's still there—the desire to have someone close. Hidden behind the fears is a little hope that someone will come along and take me out of the fears—a woman with empathy. Another part of me is

afraid she won't be understanding, and won't accept
me as I am. Human beings are all isolates, but
reaching out and touching another person is the most
profound sexual truth!

I can still hear the emotion in his voice, and I'm glad I
swallowed the "you look terrific" and "the right woman will
come along" platitudes that were pushing their way into my
consciousness because I had no answer for him.

If we are sexual beings to the end of our lives, then
where are we to take this very precious and uniquely personal
gift? Who will be the receivers of our affection, companionship, our touching and baring of innermost selves, our sharing
of those parts which happen to be genital, our remembrance
of our own sexual history? Who will hear us, touch us, and be
pleased that we touch them—with words or hands or
eyes—when we are old?

Heterosexual Affection

In a communal living setting for elderly in Evanston,
Illinois, the average age is 82. The women, of course,
outnumber the men, and when Oscar (referred to as
"everybody's darling") died it was particularly difficult (Wax,
1976). For some he was father, for others surrogate husband
or indulged brother—even rumored suitor of one woman.
This woman described her relationship with Oscar as "a little
hand-holding," and glowing, "a little kissing." I am aware of
the many facets of Oscar's manhood—the richness of his
sexuality which allowed him so many different relationships
with his friends, from father to brother to lover. Contrast
Oscar's experience with the words of five older people (aged
68 to 87) who were videotaped as they expressed their
differing sexual attitudes and experiences:

"Sexuality is a thing of the past"
"There are other ways of expressing love besides sex"
"Women stop thinking about sex at 60 or 65"
"Men lose their sexuality about age 80, but women don't ever"
"We had sexual intercourse much longer than most—up to age 81"
"I haven't slept with a man for over 11 years. . . my health is so
    poor I wouldn't want to burden any man with my health"
"What I miss is a soft shoulder"

"After they took my prostate gland out I didn't have any more sexual
desire. . . until just this spring!" (87 year old)
"I miss someone washing my back"
"I don't suppose I've had sex in 25 years, and I don't know
if I could or I couldn't"
"Venereal disease, and fear of venereal disease, is a problem"
"A man should be the forward one! We [women] couldn't even kiss
on the first date."

These five people shared that companionship and compassion
were most important to them now and echoed the feeling of
being starved for affection (all were widows or widowers).
They affirmed that Rollo May's (1969) "when you love a
little you die a little" was true for them, and voiced the
conflict between freedom and privacy versus loneliness. They
responded positively to seeing themselves on the playback of
the videotape, with candidness and increased desire to talk
about human sexuality resulting. I believe that new behaviors
emerge as older people see and hear themselves say aloud
what they normally leave unspoken. Some grief was
expressed by the group that they would not be able to find
people to talk about sexuality with again.

Judith Wax's (1975) interview with 74 year old Celia in
"Sex and the Single Grandparent" provides a different
glimpse:

> Sex isn't as powerful a need as when you're young,
> but the whole feeling is there; it's as nice as it ever
> was. He puts his arms around you, kisses you, and it
> comes to you—satisfaction and orgasm—just like it
> always did. . .don't let anybody tell you different.
> Maybe it only happens once every two weeks, but as
> you get older it's such a release from the tensions. I'm
> an old dog who's even tried a few new tricks. Like
> oral sex, for instance. . .We weren't too crazy about it
> though. . . . we take baths together and he washes my
> body and I wash his. I know I'm getting old and my
> skin could use an ironing, but we love each other—so
> sex is beautiful. (p. 46-47)

For functional people who can choose sexual expression,
options and decisions seem clearer than when memory loss is

evident, and our tendencies to childize old people go unthwarted. Judith Wax (1975) provides another case study:

> Sometimes when mind and memory suffer loose connections, feeling can still send a message through. When Becky and Barney, both in their eighties, arrived at the retirement hotel their children found for them...both were lost and apathetic. They (became) blissfully inseparable since their mutual discovery three years ago... "They go up at night together," said the social director. "They neck in the theater, they help one another on the potty." ... "Barney's children think their father has deteriorated because of Becky...They need more care now than they'd get here, but they'd probably die without each other." At the insistence of Barney's children, however, the couple was dispatched to separate nursing homes. "Let's face it," said the social director, "Barney's kids just don't like the girl he goes with." (p. 47)

An incident of sexual touching occurred in a nursing home where a colleague and I were conducting an observational study. This was a warm exchange of hands on knees, thighs, and stomach by two wheelchair residents. The woman had appeared "out of touch" with reality before and after this exchange. This was the most alive behavior observed between this man and woman in a three-month period of weekly observations. I agree with Wax (1975) that "when the circus is nearly over, one last swing—two on the trapeze—is a thrilling, death-defying act. There is, after all, no retirement age for the feeling heart." (p. 47)

If our goal for institutional residents is superior functioning at the end of life, given their limited physical and psychological energy reserves, we need to look at maximizing their energy potential through sensual-sexual exchange. And if this appears to be a rather large and frightening order for staff, family and friends of the aged, we can begin by visualizing how we might meet the human needs of the woman who said "what I miss is a soft shoulder," and of the man who said, "since my wife died I don't have anyone to wash my back."

Sexual Choice Without Societal Punishment

Compare your definition of homosexuality with one given in *The Hite Report* (1976):

> . . . the desire to be physically intimate with someone of one's own sex at some time, or always, during one's life, can be considered a natural and "normal" variety of life experience. It is "abnormal" only when you posit as "normal" and "healthy" only an interest in reproductive sex.

An ad in a porno magazine implied great risk: "Elderly Lesbian grandmother desires companion to share expenses and travel to Vancouver." It is tragically limiting that this ad probably could appear few places except in a porno magazine. What fantasies did the words bring to your mind? Stay with those images for a moment and then re-read the definition given above.

A lesbian colleague on a staff where I formerly worked has shared that it takes an increasing toll to remain "in the closet." to conceal her sexual identity, as she ages. She believes that paranoia about sexual identity increases with age, and the diminished life energy reserves which every woman faces in the aging process are tied up in concealment of sexual identity. (Age killing us softly again!)

In a large nursing home one resident became uptight about another woman who very frequently touched and held hands, as well as hugged, other female residents. The "hugger" was a warm, tender, and uninhibited person who appeared to accept her body deterioration with equanimity. The "uptight" woman was successful in her smear campaign against the affectionate woman, who became socially ostracized. This can happen....but only with support from whoever has the power—in the agency, institution, hospital or office—to collude with our vicious and dehumaniziang sexual myths.

Consider these words of a young gay woman as she projects life forty years ahead with her chosen partner:

> Ann, you and I are so blessed to still have each other. Forty years together! Can it be that long? It's still as nice as ever to snuggle up with you in bed or exchange a hug and kiss as we pass each other in the

kitchen. And our gentle, easy lovemaking is as good as ever. As a matter of fact, it seems that the older we've gotten the more time we've had to enjoy sex. Physiologically we lesbians have an advantage over other older women—clitoral stimulation and response don't change with aging. I'm certainly glad I'm gay.

I'm also glad we made the decision, so long ago now, not 'to hide.' Sure, we've faced a lot of discrimination and abuse by being open, but it released so much energy for other things. And it vastly increased the number of people with whom we could share all of our lives. I must admit that after all these years a disgusted look or cold reception still hurts some.

One lesbian professional pointed out how words distort human experience. In the 1977 NBC TV national news special on homosexuality, the term "practicing homosexuals" was used. This smacks of the disease model—something to be "cured of," for we don't speak of "practicing heterosexuals." If we expect older gay people to transcend their fears we need to sift through our words, nuances of gesture, facial expression, and bodily avoidance.

This very positive woman told me further that gay women face restricted life choices and options earlier than heterosexual women do, and need to depend on a solid sense of their own identity earlier in life. They do not face, for example, the identity crisis of the middle-years woman who has depended on her husband and children for definition of self. Many unmarried and childless women time their lives in terms of families they might have had and the main events of life developmental stages which affect the whole culture, according to Greenleigh (1974). Women who have preferred same-sexed partners are still surrounded by the aging experiences of empty nest, loss of partner, lack of younger friends, and lack of family at the end of life.

Gay people who have disappointed their families by their sexual preference are even frustrated in planning for their estates. Some people invest in life insurance to prevent families from contesting their wills. Lack of legal "related-ness" causes other problems for partners:

Mary and I bought our home as a protection for our old age so we'd never be displaced. But we hadn't taken into account the state inheritance laws. We were technically unrelated, but I was the 'widowed' survivor in joint tenancy. Since I couldn't prove I had actually made 50% of the house payments and contributed 50% of our assets when she died, the law assessed an inheritance tax on the total value of our holdings, including the half that was rightfully mine to begin with. Our savings account was depleted after Mary's long illness, so I had to sell our home to pay the taxes.

As one lesbian put it, "You can't count on the institutions— the church, the law, the family—so you have to plan better for your own life!"

Kathy Boyle of the Lesbian Resource Center in Seattle distinguishes two categories of older lesbian women: those able to take care of themselves in society who have no need for sharing their sexual identity with non-lesbians; and women institutionalized who must remain in the closet because they are so dependent on staff, professionals, and socialization with peers that they cannot risk disclosing who they are. We who work with older people may create added pain for this last group of people. Kathy explained that these older women have spent so many years receiving no support from society for who they are that their risk and trust levels are extremely low. Illness, immobility, and aloneness add to the burden of guarding their identity. To outwardly risk expressing affection and to court rejection for who one has been all one's life requires more energy than older lesbian women may be able to give.

Heterosexual women are now having to come to terms with two or three spouses to love, leave or be left by, and to grieve over—rather than the one life-partner which was customary in our older-old generation today. Homosexual women were told historically that "gay relationships don't last," and therefore many have learned to deal with grief, loss, and beginning again. These women have something to teach their heterosexual sisters in terms of learning to live with successive partners. It is unfortunate that fear keeps older women of different sexual preferences from sharing these kinds of deep human learnings. The combined impact of the women's movement and the gay women's movement have elevated the identity of all older women.

Check your own personal biases as you read these very differing responses to three "all gay people are. . ." myths:

1. Older lesbian women have more choice of partners because there are more older women than men.

> If I were 60 right now, I'd still have a harder time finding a partner because lesbians are not identifiable, and we — like all women — have been socialized not to approach people. Initiating is hard . . . what if I fall in love with a straight and she rejects me?

> The energetic, social, coping older lesbian woman has as many choices as younger gay women because lesbians are not as hung-up on youth and beauty standards. What I look for in a partner is an interesting, intelligent woman with some common interests.

2. Homosexuals, like heterosexuals, suffer from agism and the double standard of aging.

> The double standard of aging reverses itself for gay men, and is extremely painful. The mid-years over-the-hill syndrome may begin very early for homosexual men, who face fewer and fewer partners as their youth-focused image of physical attractiveness declines.

> Aging doesn't affect lesbian feminists as much as it does women caught up in the 'outer shell' definition of beauty. Lesbians are increasingly honoring older women, using them as role-models, and asking them to teach younger women how to grow old.

3. Older gay people have learned to deal with the heterosexual world and no longer mind being in the minority.

> A gay person of any age is negated every day by heterosexual assumptions — jokes, slurs, the emphasis on male-female productivity in sex.

A sensitive staff member started to serve orange juice to an older lesbian woman we were visiting. Suddenly she stopped herself and said to us, 'I'm going to check if this is from Florida — I know you wouldn't want that!' Taking very seriously what our feelings might be about Anita Bryant's crucifixion of gays, she returned shortly with, 'It's all right — it's from California!' She showed an appreciation of who we were.

We need to look at our personal sexual stereotypes and how they hinder communication. We need to look at the ways in which we approach men and women which disallow their unique sexual identity. In what ways do we offend? How do we cut off any possible communication to us about the life history of the person we're seeking to know?

These two quotations from *The Hite Report* (1976) point to some of the issues in sexual expression between any two persons:

My best sex experiences were with my woman friend because . . . the opportunity to act the aggressor . . . was wonderful; lovemaking was so mutual, endless, unhurried . . . she didn't quickly tighten up into a ball of sweat and demand the old in and out . . . I didn't worry about coming, there was no program. . . I didn't worry about my body, whether it was 'adequate.'

I have had many sexual experiences with men, and found them satisfying. However, eighteen years ago (I am sixty-six now) I met Sarah. When she announced she loved me and proceeded to demonstrate it, there was no further need for men. I feel my sex life is as complete now as it ever was . . . Ours is no 'male-female' relationship, but a sharing of everything with mutual respect.

I'm increasingly finding that young women who are physically disabled hold many clues for us in being more creative and more sensitive to the sexual experiences of older women. Listen to these words from a pamphlet on intimacy for physically disabled women.

The gender of the person I love is really irrelevant to me . . . but my disability doesn't limit me . . . With

women, loving is much less acrobatic . . . I guess I just
feel that my disability is more O.K. with women.

I prefer to relate sexually to women because they are
far less judgmental of my 'odd' body, and really far
more into sensual expression than men.

What many people have to say to me is that body image
is terribly important in being able to express oneself sexually
and sensually, and that women and gay men do fear men's
rejection if they are imperfect — particularly as they age.
And, just as importantly, that men need more help in
expressing and receiving tenderness, over-all body sensuality,
and sensitivity to the whole world of sexualness outside of
erection-producing. For older men sensory awareness offers a
wonderful alternative to the four letter word which has
guided their behaviors and fantasies for too many years. To
die softly to sensory, sensual and sexual touch — before one
is dead — is an unnecessary cruelty to the human mind, body
and spirit!

I share with you now a continuum of sexual options and
relationship to life energy which I have developed for older
people in sexuality training. The purpose is for us to see
where we might be at this point in our lives, and to stretch
our boundaries — as much as feels comfortable to us — in
order to envision new ways of being from now to the end of
life.

O P T I O N S	Denying sexual feelings & identity	Completing grief work; laying past sexual history to rest	Creative remembering of past identity	Sharing affection to extent chosen	Risking new relationship to fullness possible in current life situation
E N E R G Y	Diminished energy, tied up in withholding identity from self, others	Grief work frees energy to invest in other areas of life	Energy sources tapped through access to past sexual identity	New energy sources	New energy; new trust level developed; risk of new identity and pain, as well as joy

Summary

I have shared some of my insights concerning the double-bind of agism and sexism, as it affects men as well as women. I have also shared some aging and aged people and experiences, and hopefully pointed to the blurry distinctions which do not always hold water and which separate us needlessly in the deep gulf of human sexuality. I hope I have communicated that if we begin to see the older people we work with as sexual beings — past, present or future — and do not cloud our eyes with what their possibilities for change are, then they will have something to respond to!

Will you now consider, in the privacy of your own sexual filter, the following questions. If you should feel emotions rising up inside you at some point, jot down that question to ask yourself again later. You may want to get input from an older friend, colleague, relative or staff member. After you have plumbed the issues for any meaning they have for you, you may wish to share the questions with the populations you work with. (Be aware that you may be shaping, in your mind's eye, new options for your own aging.)

Questions

(1) What does "old" mean to you? What picture do you see?

(2) In what ways do you affirm and give permission for other people to be themselves, to widen their sexual options? (Be aware of your eyes, body movement, tone of voice, words, hesitancy, body stance.)

(3) How have you learned to accept your body — to be at peace with the body in which you live — so you can relax with your own limitations, and enjoy your own sexuality and that of others?

(4) What are your strengths in helping other people who are at war with their bodies *re-own* the parts of their bodies, minds, and feelings that they've disowned with aging?

(5) Do you have difficulty in touching older people? In what ways do you touch them, and what does it mean to you? (Sensory? Affectional? Sexual?

Other?) Do you ask the other person what the meaning is for them, so communication is clear between you?

(6) What fears — if any — are you in touch with when you relate to someone of a different sexual preference than your own? In what ways do you attempt to see the *person* behind the sexual preference?

(7) How do you non-verbally honor or dishonor the sexual preferences of people who are: ugly, heterosexual, asexual, attractive, gay, lesbian, disabled, bisexual, ill? (Add other "categories" of people that blind us to personhood.)

(8) In what ways do you think about — and affirm — your own parents' sexuality, if you do. How does this affect your openness to older people's sexuality, and to your own?

These questions may be used in a staff meeting or group with deep breathing and relaxation to help focus in the beginning. Allow participants to close their eyes and be very comfortable, to consider each question with considerable time for silence in between, and the choice of writing responses afterward if they wish. The group discussion which follows is often more meaningful when each person has had an opportunity to internalize and reflect. These questions are a parting gift, a tool for widening your own sensory-sensual-sexual horizons.

Wilhelm Reich cited the release of sexual energy through a healthy sexual life as a criterion for mental health (Raknes, 1976). Victor Kassel says, "It's a well-established fact that for many people sexual orgasm brings immediate relief from anxiety. It's also a fact that most patients in nursing homes suffer from chronic anxiety." (Horn, 1974) I close with Reich's injunction to a sex life chosen by the older person without discrimination or punishment:

> Each individual — child, youth, adult, and old person — has the right to a sex life corresponding to his or her need, when this need does not conflict with the right of other people to their own person. (Raknes, 1976, p. 174)

Age need not "kill us softly." It can, instead, be a new beginning of relatedness and self-identity for those who choose.

References

Broverman, I. K., Broverman, D. M., Clarkson, F. E., Rosenkrantz, P. S., & Vogel, S. R. Sex role stereotypes and clinical judgments of mental health. *Journal of Consulting and Clinical Psychiatry,* 1970, *34*(1), 1-7.

Calderone, M. S. The sexuality of aging. *Siecus Newsletter,* 1971, 7(1). (October)

de Beauvoir, S. *The coming of age.* New York: G. P. Putnam's Sons, 1972.

Genevay, B., & Rounds, K. Touching behaviors in a nursing home environment. Unpublished paper, 1974.

Greenleigh, L. Facing the challenge of change in middle age. *Geriatrics,* November 1974, p. 63.

Hite, S. *The Hite report.* New York: Dell, 1976.

Horn, P., and the Editors of *Behavior Today.* Rx: Sex for senior citizens. *Psychology Today,* June 1974, pp. 18-20.

Long, I. Human sexuality and aging. *Social Casework,* 1976, *57*(4), 237-243.

May, R. *Love and will.* New York: W. W. Norton, 1969.

Rainer, J., & Rainer, J. *Sexual adventure in marriage.* New York: Simon & Schuster, 1965.

Raknes, O. *Wilhelm Reich and orgonomy.* Baltimore: Penguin, 1976.

Rockey, L. Human sexuality teacher. *The Seattle Times Magazine,* March 28, 1976, p. 4.

Sontag, S. The double standard of aging. *Saturday Review, The Society,* September 23, 1972.

Task Force on Concerns of Physically Disabled Women. Toward intimacy: Family planning and sexuality concerns of physically disabled women. Everett, Washington: Planned Parenthood of Snohomish County, Washington, Inc., 1977.

Wax, J. It's like your own home here. *The New York Times Magazine,* November 21, 1976.

Wax, J. Sex and the single grandparent. *New Times,* September 19, 1975, pp. 43-47.

Sexuality in the Aging Individual 3

Eric Pfeiffer

For all too long, aging persons were believed not to have any sexual feelings, and certainly no longer to be participant in an active sexual life. If these assumptions were in fact correct, then practicing physicians need not concern themselves either with sexual feelings or sexual activity among their aging patients.

But the facts are really quite otherwise (Brotman, 1973). On the positive side, sexual interest and activity continue to play a significant and sometimes a major role in the continuing life satisfactions available to the aging. On the negative side, a host of problems related to sexual expression in the later years do vex and trouble some older people, either temporarily or continually. As in the younger years, aging persons, too, will turn to physicians to seek help with these problems.

The question for us will be whether we are ready to respond to this call for help on the part of our aging patients.

In order to be able to respond adequately, physicians must be equipped with appropriate attitudinal sets and adequate factual information regarding the physiology, sociology, and psychology of sexual behavior in the later years.

Attitudinal Sets

Attitudinally, physicians need to understand that aging patients retain their right to sexual expression, if need be in altered form and in altered settings, and that they also retain their right to ask for and receive professional counsel when they encounter difficulties in their legitimate pursuits for satisfying sexual expression. It is quite clear that many physicians and other health care personnel share with the rest of society a distinct taboo regarding sexual expression on the part of aging individuals. This may relate in part to our own upbringing in a society which, although it has become liberated for all other segments of society in terms of sexual expression, still retains certain Victorian standards regarding sexual expression by older persons. In part this taboo is related to feelings which all of us harbor regarding sexual expression in our parent generation, and more specifically in our own parents. Our aging patients may remind us to a significant degree of our own parents, and as such we may wish to avoid dealing with the sexuality of elderly people.

Nevertheless, however timid and tentative we as professionals may feel about the sexual needs of the elderly, they themselves usually are not at all reluctant to discuss this area of their lives with a professional, and they clearly welcome the physician who is comfortable and capable of dealing with this intimate area of their lives.

This is true for an aging population which was born around the turn of the century, which grew up in the 1910's, 1920's, or at the latest, the 1930's. It may be even more strikingly so for future generations of the aging. As people are living longer they are interested in the extension not only of the duration of life but of the quality of life. If sexual expression contributes to the quality of life in the younger and adult years, is it not reasonable to assume that it should continue to do so in the later years?

Some Facts About Physiology,
Psychology and Sociology

Dr. William Masters has done extensive work on the changed physiology of sexual expression in the later years (Busse & Pfeiffer, 1969). His basic findings are extremely encouraging. First, there appears to be no biologic limitation to sexual capacity in the aging female. In the aging male there are some substantial changes in the degree of completeness of erectile capacity, a slowing of the time to ejaculation, and less forceful ejaculation. These changes, however, do not need to contribute substantially to diminution of satisfactory sexual expression in aging men. With the exception of specific existing diseases, physiologic changes do not ring a mandatory curtain on sexuality in either aging men or aging women.

Some of our research at the Duke University Center for the Study of Aging and Human Development has indicated that approximately 80 percent of aging men (average age, 68 years) continue to be interested in sex (Busse & Pfeiffer, 1973). Most intriguingly, even in the age decade 68-78, almost none of them lose their interest. The proportion of men who at age 60 are still sexually active on any regular basis is only moderately decreased. About 70 percent of elderly men still are regularly sexually active at age 68, but by the time they reach age 78 the proportion has declined to about 25 percent. Still, 1 of 4 men aged 78 or older is still regularly sexually active. Moreover longitudinal researches on some of these subjects indicated that not only is continued sexual activity possible or even probable, but for a small but significant proportion there is an increase in sexual expression over a period of ten years. This finding was certainly astonishing if not heartening to researchers and others (Leaf, 1973).

In addition we found that there was no decade this side of 100 years in which there were no individuals who had continued to be sexually active. In short, sex is not confined to sexagenarians but can be a continuing activity for septuagenarians, octogenarians and even nonagenarians. We personally did not study any centenarians, but from a review of the literature and some of the reports like those from Dr.

Alexander Leaf and others who have studied groups of centenarians, biology has not established a mandatory age for sexual retirement (Leaf, 1973).

Another important finding from our studies is that the likelihood of continued sexual expression in the later years is substantially greater for persons who have been highly interested and highly sexually active in their younger years (Masters & Johnson, 1966). Thus there is no basis for the contention that "you can wear it out." Rather, the contrary seems true. Persons who have been very active in their younger years tend to continue their sexual expression into the later decades of their lives.

Along social and demographic lines, however, we ran into some significant problems. As far as men are concerned, marital status makes absolutely no difference in regard to sexual expression. Married men as a group do not differ from unmarried men as a group in the degree of sexual activity (Pfeiffer, 1969). On the other hand, for women marital status seems to make all the difference. Very few unmarried women reported any degree of regular sexual activity in the later years. The unavailability of a societally sanctioned sexual partner was the principal determinant for the discontinuation of sexual activity on the part of many women. The ratio of available older men to available older women is truly astonishing. At age 65 there are 129 women for every 100 men; by age 75 the ratio is 156 women for every 100 men (Pfeiffer, 1974). But that is not nearly the end of the story. Most of the men at this age will be married and more than half of the women will be unmarried. As a more concrete demonstration of the imbalance of numbers, let me tell you about one housing project for the elderly in a nearby city. The residents were 375 people aged 65 or older — 75 men and 300 women, for a ratio of 400:100. But the story does not end there. Seventy-three of these men were married; only 2 were unmarried. That leaves 2 available men for 227 women. Thus although biology may not limit the sexual capabilities of aging women it does restrict their opportunities for sexual expression through the limits biology sets on the survival of males. As physicians we must be concerned not only with encouraging or permitting the continued sexual participation of men and women who are still married and have sexual partners available, but also with non-partnered elderly persons who continue to share these same needs.

Implications for Practice

Some clinicians have observed that in old age, which elsewhere I have described as a season of loss, e.g., of jobs, friends, spouses, and participation in community affairs (Pfeiffer & Davis, 1972), sexual needs may not only be continuing but actually be heightened due to the losses in other areas of life. How should the clinician respond?

Any response on the part of the clinician should be geared to a respect for the continuation of lifestyle for every aged person. I am not suggesting that clinicians whip older people into some kind of a sexual frenzy or instill new or uncongenial patterns of sexual expression into their aging patients. Rather I am counseling the desirability of encouraging and assuring continuity of sexual expression for those for whom this has constituted an important part of their lives in the past. A number of intercurrent illnesses, physical or psychologic, can *temporarily* lead to a decrease or even disappearance of sexual expression. Myocardial infarction on the physical side and a depressive reaction on the psychologic side are excellent examples of factors which may *interrupt* the capacity, or the wisdom, or the desire for sexual expression (Pfeiffer, Verwoerdt & Wang, 1969). However, the physician should be aware that these need be only *temporary* interruptions, rather than causes for permanent cessation of sexual expression in all cases. Once a myocardial infarction has healed, there is no reason why the cardiac patient should not return to regular sexual expression, unless he is so severely impaired that he cannot tolerate even modest exercise of any kind. Once a depressive reaction has been treated, whether psychologically or pharmacologically, the patient may need to be informed that his decline in sexual activity was a manifestation of his depressive reaction, not of his advancing age.

I have seen many aging couples who have given great pleasure to each other through continued sexual expression. Who wants to rob anyone of this opportunity?

Sexual expression requires *privacy*. For our elderly we often provide adequate physical medical care, good shelter and clothing and good living arrangements, with this one possible exception. Many living arrangements do not provide for adequate privacy for older persons. This is true whether the older people are living with their adult relatives or whether they are residing in institutions such as nursing homes or homes for the aged. If these facilities are to be homes, privacy must be assured. If privacy is assured, then opportunity for sexual expression is also assured. Because many elderly persons are non-partnered, there must be greater acceptance by physicians of solitary sexual expression, and this acceptance should be conveyed to patients and to other care-givers as well as to family members. We have a lot of public educating to do in this regard.

There is always the possibility of re-marriage. Substantial research has indicated that re-marriage in the later years has an excellent chance of being emotionally, socially, and economically satisfying, in addition to extending the likelihood of survival of both participants. Especially for elderly persons who have had reasonably satisfactory marriages in their younger years, re-marriage is desirable. There is one caution in this regard. In order to be successful, re-marriage ought to be between individuals who share a common set of values. Thus the widow of a former college president probably should not marry the widowed plumber, but persons from similar backgrounds make excellent new partners, companions, and lovers for those who have been deprived of their lifelong partners. Sexual expression is one reason for getting married, but it is one of many reasons.

Sexual expression should be considered in the overall context of successful aging (Pfeiffer, Verwoerdt & Wang, 1968). Examination of all the available data makes it clear that successfully aging persons are those who have made a decision to stay in training in major areas of their lives. In particular, they have decided to stay in training physically, socially, emotionally and intellectually. We have every reason to believe that staying in training sexually also will help to improve the quality of life in the later years.

References

Brotman, H. E. Who are the aging? In E. W. Busse & E. Pfeiffer (Eds.), *Mental illess in later life.* Washington: American Psychiatric Association, 1973.

Busse, E. W., & Pfeiffer, E. *Behavior and adaptation in later life.* Boston: Little, Brown, 1969.

Busse, E. W., & Pfeiffer, E. *Mental illness in later life.* Washington: American Psychiatric Association, 1973.

Leaf, A. Every day is a gift when you are over 100. *National Geographic,* 1973, *143,* 93.

Masters, W. H., & Johnson, V. E. *Human sexual response.* Boston: Little, Brown, 1966.

Pfeiffer, E. Sexual behavior in old age. In E. W. Busse and E. Pfeiffer (Eds.), *Behavior and adaptation in late life.* Boston: Little, Brown, 1969.

Pfeiffer, E. (Ed.) *Successful aging.* Durham, North Carolina: Duke University Center for the Study of Aging and Human Development, 1974.

Pfeiffer, E., & Davis, G. C. Determinants of sexual behavior in middle and old age. *Journal of the American Geriatrics Society,* 1972, *20,* 151.

Pfeiffer, E., Verwoerdt, A., & Wang, H. S. The natural history of sexual behavior in a biologically advantaged group of aged individuals. *Journal of Gerontology,* 1969, *24,* 193.

Pfeiffer, E., Verwoerdt, A., & Wang, H. S. Sexual behavior in aged men and women. I. Observations on 254 community volunteers. *Archives of General Psychiatry,* 1968, *19,* 641.

Footnotes

[1] Reprinted with permission, from *Journal of the American Geriatrics Society,* 1974, *22*(11), 481-484.

Sexual Responsiveness, Age, and Change: Facts and Potential

Robert L. Solnick

There seems to be little doubt that sexual responsiveness does change with advancing years for both the male and female. The important issue, however, is whether or not these changes must necessarily lead to a net loss in the person's sexual functioning. The changes in responsiveness can be measured in a scientific manner, and part of this chapter will be devoted to reviewing and commenting on these changes. However, viewing these changes in a perjorative manner may imply that one has invoked a value system which overlooks the potential positive aspects of the change. Since value systems are strongly culturally determined, a reassessment of one's values may make it possible to utilize the change as a motivating factor in moving toward a growth experience. The degree to which this can be accomplished will depend almost entirely on the personality and level of motivation of the individual.

We often are prone to emphasize the loss aspect of the changes which occur with advancing age, sexual as well as otherwise, without due regard for the potential gain which may be inherent in some of these changes. Schwartz and

Mensh (1974) pointed out that "the process of aging is inextricably linked to change, and that many, if indeed not most, such changes may be placed into the matrix of loss." They go on to recommend that the negative effect of these losses may be minimized by compensating for the losses. In a way, one might interpret the remarks of this chapter in a compensatory framework, but that seems to have a certain negative flavor. It would appear preferable to think of the changes as a signal which alerts the person to reevaluate the basis on which he or she has been functioning in that particular area. The sexual area is one which, in the author's opinion, lends itself well to this kind of potential growth experience. To a great extent this is due to the rather narrow boundaries that our culture has set for the sexual behavior, particularly for the generations which are currently in the middle and later years.

It should be obvious, of course, that it is very difficult, if not impossible, to interpret certain changes as anything but a loss. It would be naive and unrealistic to take the position, for example, that the loss of one's eyesight would be an opportunity for a growth experience. It is true that a person could experience some growth, even in this tragic situation, but, on balance, one would have to acknowledge this as a serious loss. Unfortunately, there are many such changes that may occur with increasing age, and Schwartz and Mensh's (1974) compensatory model is a positive way of dealing with these losses. It is the author's contention that in the sexual arena, the balance sheet may indicate a net gain rather than a net loss.

The Evidence Relative to Change

There is considerable evidence that sexual responsiveness does decline for both the male and female throughout their adult lives (Kinsey, Pomeroy & Martin, 1948; Kinsey, Pomeroy, Martin & Gebhard, 1953; Masters & Johnson, 1966; Solnick & Birren, 1977). In addition, there is some evidence that the rate of change seems to accelerate as one moves from the late forties into the early fifties (Masters & Johnson, 1966; Pfeiffer, Verwoerdt & Davis, 1972; Solnick, 1977). First, some of the experimental evidence relative to the changes in male erectile responsiveness will be presented (Solnick, 1977; Solnick & Birren, 1977).

Male Erectile Response

Although Masters and Johnson (1966) had previously observed that men moving into their 50's required a considerably longer time to attain an erection than men in their 20's, their subject population was rather an unusual group. They were mostly couples who, after some indoctrination into the experimental procedure, were capable of engaging in sexual intercourse in the presence of experimenters and cameras. As a step toward minimizing this effect, a study (Solnick & Birren, 1977) was conducted to quantitatively evaluate the difference in response of a group of young men (19-30 years) and a group of older men (48-65 years) who had been selected from a more general population.

To accomplish this purpose, two groups of ten subjects, each in the appropriate age categories, were solicited from the personnel roles of the University of Southern California. At the time of solicitation, they were not aware of the nature of the experiment; of those who expressed an interest in participating, 78% accepted after being informed about the details of the study. This high acceptance rate made it less likely that those who did become subjects did not do so because of the sexual nature of the study. Since details of the experiment have been presented elsewhere (Solnick & Birren, 1977), only a brief outline of the procedure and results will be presented here.

A penile plethysmograph (Karacan, 1969) was used to continuously record the actual erectile response of each subject in both age groups as they observed a ten minute erotic movie. The experiment was conducted in total privacy, and the subjects were nude below the waist. Questionnaires and test instruments were used as means of evaluating any physiological, psychological, or anxiety problems that the subject may have been experiencing before, during, and after the experiment. Rating scales were used to determine if both the young and old group perceived the film as being equally arousing.

The results indicated that the mean rate of maximum penile circumference increase was almost 6 times more rapid for the 19-30 year old group than it was for the 48-65 year old group. This difference was significant, $t(18) = 4.70$, $p <$ .002. By comparison, Masters and Johnson (1966) stated that the rapid reaction time of the young male adult "is at least doubled and frequently trebled as the individual male passes through his fifties and into the 60 and 70 year age status" (p. 251). The greater difference between the young and old group found in the Solnick and Birren (1977) study may be explained by the previously mentioned special character of the Masters and Johnson (1966) sample, since all their subjects may have been relatively more sexually sophisticated. However, another explanation could be that it was more critical for the older men to have a live partner than it was for the younger men, even though both groups rated the erotic film to be equally arousing. But on the other side of the scale, one might expect the younger group of Masters and Johnson to find their partner to be more arousing than the partner of the older group. This is particularly true if Masters and Johnson's (1966) strong statements relative to monotony are, indeed, valid. If monotony is a crucial issue, one would expect this effect to increase the difference between the younger and older groups. In any event, it is clear that there is a decrease in erectile response rate as the male ages; the difference in findings is a matter of degree.

Another important finding in the Solnick and Birren (1977) study concerned the much more labile character of the young men's erectile profile compared to the older men's profile. The younger men responded rapidly to a particular scene in the movie that was appealing to them, then partially lost the erection, only to respond rapidly to another scene. In general, the older men tended to experience a more gradual, steady increase in erectile response which never reached the maximum levels of erection attained by the younger men. The older men also were slower to rebound from a partial loss in erection when such a decline did occur. It was as if the resiliency of the erectile system had been reduced. It should be remembered that this was not true of every older man, but rather it was true on the average. Likewise, individual younger men also had varying degrees of resiliency in their responses. There is probably no human behavior which is more idiosyncratic than that of sexual response.

Modification of Erectile Response Rate Change

Since this chapter deals with change, it seems only logical that change in either a positive or negative direction should be considered. Sviland (1975), for example, has been engaged in research and application of treatment processes relative to bringing about positive changes in sexual responsiveness. The author had some particular interest in investigating the possibility of reversing the decrease in erectile responsiveness (Solnick, 1977) which was discussed earlier (Solnick & Birren, 1977). To this end a study was conducted recently (Solnick, 1977) which set about to demonstrate that the erectile responsiveness of the middle-aged male could be modified. My particular interest centered around the role that fantasy may play in sexual behavior.

The specific purpose of this research was to test experimentally the following hypotheses: (a) The erectile response and level of sexual activity of middle-aged males will increase following a period of fantasy training and practice. (b) The increase in the level of sexual activity will persist for a period of at least two weeks following the termination of the training and practice period. (c) Feedback of the erectile response changes (biofeedback) will potentiate the effectiveness of the fantasy practice, i.e., a group receiving biofeedback will show greater response improvement than will a group that does not receive biofeedback.

The subjects for this study were 20 employees of the University of Southern California who were in the 45 to 55 year age bracket. They were chosen in the same manner as described in the previously presented study (Solnick & Birren, 1977). The acceptance rate of those who responded to the letter was 75% after they had been informed about the nature of the experiment.

The 20 subjects were divided into two experimental groups, the only difference between the groups being that one group received feedback of their physiological erectile response (the biofeedback group [BOF]) and the other group did not (the non-biofeedback group [NBOF]). The mean ages of the NBOF and BOF groups were 51.4 and 50.5 years respectively.

There were eight dependent variables included in the experiment; three of them were physiological measures and five of them were self-report measures. The three physiological measures were: (a) maximum rate of increase of penile diameter (responsiveness), (b) latency (time in seconds from exposure to an erotic stimulus to the first erectile response), and (c) maximum penile diameter increase. The five self-report measures were: (a) frequency of intercourse, (b) frequency of sexual approach to a partner, (c) frequency of erection to fantasy, (d) imagery score, and (e) daydreaming score.

The measurement of penile diameter increase, rate of diameter increase, and latency were accomplished with the penile plethysmograph mentioned previously. An audible tone, which varied in frequency as a function of the degree of erection, was used to feed the penile response information back to the subjects in the BOF group. The measurement of the five self-report measures was made by utilizing two Sexual Functioning Questionnaires designed for this experiment, the Betts Imagery Scale (Sheehan, 1967), and the Imaginal Process Inventory, a series of five daydreaming scales (Singer & Antrobus, 1966).

The general plan of the experiment was as follows: (1) At the first session, each subject viewed a ten minute erotic movie, during which time his penile response was continuously recorded. (2) For the next five sessions, each subject was asked to fantasize to four types of stimuli: (a) slides, (b) tape recordings of erotic sounds, (c) erotic literature, and (d) self-generated scenes. The subject's penile response was continuously recorded during all of these sessions. Those subjects in the BOF group received audible feedback of their response level through headphones. (3) During the seventh session the subject again viewed the same erotic movie. All sessions were scheduled on an every-other-day basis except where weekends prolonged the interval. The total elapsed time required to complete the seven sessions was approximately two weeks. (4) Two weeks after the seventh session each subject returned by mail three questionnaires related to his sexual behavior, imagery, and daydreaming activity during the two weeks following the experiment. The subjects were paid $50 to participate in the experiment, and did not receive payment until all three questionnaires were returned. As in the first experiment discussed earlier the subjects were nude below the waist and the sessions were conducted in total privacy. The subject reclined on a cot and viewed the slides and movie on a back-projected screen which was in a common wall between the subject room and an adjacent room. Essentially all of the electronic instruments and equipment was contained in the second room which was occupied by the experimenter; communication with the subject was via intercom.

The major findings of this research may be briefly summarized as follows:

1. There was a significant improvement in sexual and fantasy functioning following the 2 week period of training and practice. For example, there was a 41% increase in the mean maximum rate of erectile response. The weekly rate of intercourse increased from a mean of approximately twice per week to a mean of approximately three times per week. The mean scores on the daydreaming scales increased from 34.2 to 36.9.

2. Although the mean rate of erection improved considerably more for the BOF group than it did for the NBOF group following the training and practice period (64% vs. 17% improvement respectively) this difference did not reach statistical significance. However, there were other indications that BOF was effective. Nine of the ten subjects in the BOF group judged that the feedback of their erectile response was helpful. Also, a chi-square test of seven questions from the Sexual Functioning Questionnaires indicated that the BOF group responded affirmatively significantly more often than did the NBOF group, X^2 (1) = 14.64, p < .001. An affirmative response to these questions indicated an improvement in sexual functioning.

3. There still was a significant improvement in the subjects' sexual fantasy behavior, as measured by

the questionnaires, two weeks after the conclusion of the training and practice period.

4. The correlation between the increase in the daydreaming frequency scores and the increase in the mean maximum rate of erection was significant, r(18) = .625, p < .01. This significant correlation of fantasy increase and erectile responsiveness increase suggests that improved fantasy capabilities may be related to the practice effects.

To summarize, the data clearly supported the first two hypotheses and lent some support to the third hypothesis.

The conclusions and implications that may be drawn from these data are as follows: (a) Fantasy appears to have the capability of playing an important role in the sexual functioning of the middle-aged male. Given the opportunity to practice the use of fantasy and encouraged to do so, the middle-aged male seems to be capable of using it to enhance his sexual response. (b) This enhancement does not seem to be limited to the directed period of training and practice. Its effect appears to persist following this period. (c) Feedback of the male's erectile response does seem to make it easier for him to become aware of those fantasies which are most arousing to him.

Accelerating Change in the Middle Years

An interesting finding resulted when data from both of the previous studies (Solnick & Birren, 1977; Solnick, 1977) were combined. This combination of data seemed justified since the two studies were conducted under identical conditions. By splitting the 20 subjects in the 45 to 55 year age bracket into two younger and older groups of 10 subjects each, four groups of 10 subjects each were available for evaluation. The mean ages of the four groups were 23.6, 48.4, 53.5, and 53.8 years. Since the two oldest groups were so close in age, they were considered as one group with a mean age of 53.7 years. When this was done it was found that the difference in erectile responsiveness between the 48.4 and 53.7 year age groups was approximately 34% of the difference between the 23.6 and 53.7 year age groups. That is, this 5.3 year age difference accounted for 34% of the difference over the 30.1 year period rather than the 17% that would have been expected if the difference was based on a linear relationship. Although both of these studies were cross-sectional ones, if one can assume for a moment that a longitudinal study would have yielded similar data and that the changes were linear, then the results indicated that the decline in responsiveness in the 23.6 to 48.4 year interval was .28 x 10^{-3} in./sec./yr. compared to .67 x 10^{-3} in./sec./yr. for the 48.4 to 53.7 year interval. In other words, the decline in responsiveness rate during the 48.4 to 53.7 period was almost 2.5 times as great as it was during the 23.6 to 48.4 period.

This apparent acceleration of change around the age of 50 becomes more significant when one considers that it has been corroborated by findings of other researchers for both men and women. Masters and Johnson (1966) for example, observed that approximately 60% of the women in the 41-50 year age group demonstrated obvious increase in breast size during sexual arousal whereas only 22% demonstrated such enlargement in the 51-60 year age group. The sex flush was found to occur in 52% of the women in the 41-50 age group and 13% in the 51-60 year age group. For men, only 2 of 39 males past the age of 50 years were observed to develop the sex flush. Masters and Johnson (1966) give many other examples of rather abrupt changes at about age 50 years.

Pfeiffer, Verwoerdt, & Davis (1972) found that the sharpest increase in the percentage of those admitting awareness of a decline in sexual interest occured between the 45-50 group and the 51-55 group when they studied men and women ranging in age from 44 to 71 years. For the men, 51% in the 46-50 age group indicated that they were not aware of any decline, whereas only 29% were aware of no decline in the 51-55 age group. For the women, 42% in the 46-50 age group were aware of no decline compared to 22% in the 51-55 age group.

Runciman, in his chapter in this book, mentions the fact that impotency seems to increase markedly after the age of 50 for the male and continues to increase with each decade. Therapy data indicate that three out of every four impotency cases were over 50 years of age at its onset.

When the data from these various sources are considered, it appears that there may be an acceleration of the slow sexual response decline which characterizes the years 20-45. This acceleration seems to occur between the ages of 45-55. Biological, psychological, and sociological factors probably contribute to this change in decline rate. The change itself probably will not affect most persons' sexual pleasure as long as they realize that it is not unique to them, and that they can adapt to the change in a way that will assure them a long and full sex life. In fact, it is the author's contention that this period in a person's life may present them an opportunity for sexual enrichment.

Factors Influencing the Consequences of Change

It has been pointed out that physiological, psychological, and sociological factors probably play a role in the decline of sexual responsiveness as a person ages. Of these three factors it is probably safe to say that most people have least control over physiological changes. Attempts have been made to modify physiological changes by the use of hormones but this typically has been unsuccessful and unpredictable. There are, of course, cases where there is some body dysfunction which causes abnormal production of sex hormones, and these cases may respond to treatment. If a person generally is in good health and has none of the diseases which are known to influence sexual functioning (see Chapters 6 and 10), then there is very little he or she can do about changes which are physiologically based. It is important, of course, to follow a nutritious diet and to obtain adequate rest and sleep with a minimum amount of overindulgence in work, food, or activity.

The areas where most people do have an opportunity to influence the changes which are occurring in their sexual behavior are those which are psychologically and sociologically based, and probably more important than influencing the change itself is influencing the consequences of the change. It already has been demonstrated that in males, at least, change can be reversed to some degree (Solnick, 1977). However, it would seem that how one handles the change is even more critical, since it would be unlikely that the tide of change could be stemmed indefinitely. As mentioned earlier, one has the option of viewing the change as a challenge which, if met, could lead to a positive growth experience, or, if avoided, could lead to a role loss.

In order to explore the possibilities of sexual growth during mid and later life, it will be helpful to review the psychological and sociological factors which influenced the cohort group born during the years 1900 to 1930. It is necessary to discuss these two factors almost as a unit since they are so interrelated in their effect. Traditionally, sociological factors are thought of as being more related to cultural effects, and are not usually thought of in intra-psychic or individual terms as are psychological effects. Yet, the culture influences the parent and the parent molds the child, so that often it is difficult and not productive to draw a sharp line between these two viewpoints.

The cohort group under discussion was reaching maturity and forming permanent relationships principally during the years 1915 to 1945. These were the pre-Kinsey years when people who were engaging in sexual behavior which society labeled "unusual," or in even more derogatory terms, did so at the price of experiencing anxiety regarding their sexual behavior. These were the years when a few people, most of whom were probably at the higher socioeconomic levels, were reading *Ideal Marriage* by Van de Velde (1926). This book, far ahead of its time, emphasized the importance for both sexes of giving and receiving pleasure, and stressed that sex was not evil, as much of Victorian society had believed it to be. The genital kiss was sanctioned but the reader was cautioned regarding its use. Even though Van de Velde's thinking was far advanced, he still viewed sex as primarily the responsibility of the male, and only with the help of a skilled partner would the female be able to assume a more equal role in her sexual relationship. According to Van de Velde, the man "must know how to make love." Another weakness in Van de Velde's thinking, as viewed from today's perspective, was his stress on the importance of the simultaneous orgasm.

The work of Kinsey and his coworkers did a great deal to dispel some of the myths regarding sexual practices, and those who did read all or part of their research results may have experienced some growth in their sexual relations. In the same manner, those persons who became aware of the work of Masters and Johnson (1966) as well as the many other books that began to appear in the sixties may have been able to incorporate new concepts into their behavior. However, given the likelihood that the percentage of the cohort under discussion who read these books was probably small, and that the most important years in the formation of sexual patterns are the earlier ones, one can imagine that a great number of middle-aged and older adults probably have a great deal of growth potential remaining in their sexual relationships.

It would even be possible to conceive of one's sexual life in terms of Maslow's self-actualization model (Hall & Lindzey, 1970). In this model, one moves from a lower level of functioning which is determined by basic needs through a hierarchy of needs to the highest level which is primarily concerned with the development of an individual's full potential. From a sexual viewpoint, the lowest level of functioning might consist of male-initiated sex for the sole purpose of reproduction. The highest level of functioning might consist of a total sexual communion involving both partners in a trusting, loving, sharing, pleasure-seeking relationship which may or may not include coitus. In this concept of sexual development, one would move from levels which are necessary in order to maintain the species to levels which are more directed to experiencing all the sexual potential that a person may possess, i.e. to be sexually self-actualized. Since the members of the cohort under discussion are, for the most part, beyond the reproductive years, the levels of development important for them would be at the higher levels of the hierarchy.

Viewed from this perspective, becoming aware of change in both the male and female sexual response could be a signal to embark on a sexual growth program. Such a program would require that both sexes reevaluate the roles that society has set for them. In addition, it would require that persons think of sex in terms that include a great deal more than coitus. As mentioned earlier, the members of the cohort under discussion were taught to believe that the goal in every sexual encounter should be orgasm for both sexes, preferably simultaneously. Admittedly, an orgasm is a highly pleasurable experience, but it is certainly not the only pleasure that may result from sexual contact. It is the response that comes most naturally to the male in his younger years, although not so naturally for the female (Hite, 1976). However, for both the male and female the primary goal of sex has been for the male to bring himself and his partner to a climax. This is a heavy burden for both sexes to bear.

It is much more effective to take responsibility for one's own sexual pleasure and to communicate these needs to one's partner. For example, in most relationships it probably has been customary for the male to engage in a great deal of foreplay in order to prepare his partner for insertion and hopefully climax. Most women are probably accustomed to having their partner become erect during this foreplay and might find it disturbing if he did not. However, the older male may require more specific and extended stimulation than he did previously, so there may be a need for stimulation by the female. If the male is aware of this need and has sufficient trust in his partner to ask that the need be satisfied, the sexual relationship will certainly be enhanced. In a similar manner, an older woman may need to be stimulated both physically and emotionally in a different manner than when she was younger, and it is equally important that she share these needs with her partner. In both cases it is essential that both sexes take the time to become aware of their own needs as they experience changes and not place this responsibility on their partner's shoulders.

There are so many different aspects of sexuality which most middle-aged and older persons have not experienced that the potential for growth is enormous. The art of non-demanding pleasuring of each other through massage with or without the use of oils, lotions, and vibrators is only one example. Many older people have never experienced the pleasure of taking a bubble bath with their lover. Self-stimulation alone or with one's partner is another dimension of sex which many have not enjoyed. Oral-genital sex can be a highly pleasurable and loving kind of sexual experience. The sharing of fantasies and playing them out together can be very exciting. Taking the time to browse through bookstores together or alone and sharing information resulting from exposure to new information can be very rewarding. The list of potential experiences is endless, limited only by the creativity of the individuals involved.

There is much room for creative thinking and experiencing in the area of sex, particularly for those persons who were maturing during the sexually repressive years. The growth potential for most of these persons is tremendous. Change is inevitable, but the consequences of change, in large part, will be determined by how willing the person is to take a fresh look at his or her ideas concerning sexual behavior. Equally important is how willing a person is to devote the time that is necessary to become sexually self-actualized. In addition, there must be a willingness to take a certain amount of risk, which involves trusting one's partner not to take advantage of one's openness and vulnerability. Sex is a very sensitive subject, very much related to our self-concept, and therefore any admission of needs tends to place one in a vulnerable position. However, if one is willing to devote the time, think creatively, take responsibility for one's own body, and take the risk, the sexual changes that result from aging can indeed be the beginning of a new and more rewarding level of sexual functioning. The end point of this growth experience may be different from the sexual experiences of younger years, but has the potential for being even better.

References

Hall, C. S., & Lindzey, G. *Theories of personality.* New York: John Wiley, 1970.

Hite, S. *The Hite report.* New York: MacMillan, 1976.

Karacan, I. A simple and inexpensive transducer for quantitative measurements of penile erection during sleep. *Behavior Research Methods and Instruments,* 1969, *1,* 251-252.

Kinsey, A. C., Pomeroy, W. B., & Martin, C. E. *Sexual behavior in the human male.* Philadelphia: W. B. Saunders, 1948.

Kinsey, A. C., Pomeroy, W. B., Martin, C. E., & Gebhard, P. H. Sexual behavior in the human female. Philadelphia: W. B. Saunders, 1953.

Masters, W. H., & Johnson, V. E. *Human sexual response.* Boston: Little, Brown, 1966.

Pfeiffer, E., Verwoerdt, A., & Davis, G. Sexual behavior in middle life. *American Journal of Psychiatry,* 1972, *128*(10), 82-87.

Schwartz, A. N., & Mensh, I. N. *Professional obligations and approaches to the aged.* Springfield, Illinois: Charles C. Thomas, 1974.

Sheehan, P. A shortened form of Betts' questionnaire upon mental imagery. *Journal of Clinical Psychology,* 1967, *23,* 386-389.

Singer, J., & Antrobus, J. *The imaginal process inventory.* New York: City College of New York Center for Research in Cognition and Affect, 1966.

Solnick, R. L. Alteration of human male erectile response and sexual behavior. (Doctoral dissertation, University of Southern California, 1977).

Solnick, R. L., & Birren, J. E. Age and male erectile responsiveness. *Archives of Sexual Behavior,* 1977, *6*(1), 1-9.

Sviland, M. A. P. Helping elderly couples become sexually liberated: Psycho-social issues. *The Counseling Psychologist,* 1975, *5,* 67-72.

Van de Velde, T. H. *Ideal marriage.* New York: Random House, 1926.

The Physiology of Sexuality in Aging **5**

Ruth B. Weg

I'd die before I ever let myself get old.
I would always stay young.
And what did I want for my life to be?
I wanted then
the same as I want now:
everything!

To go everywhere in the world,
to be everybody in the world,
to slide under the ocean, climb over the moon
swing back and forth between them
thumbing my nose.

You think I couldn't make you a good lover still?
You're crazy if you don't think so.
I could make you miserable with anyone else.
You would close your eyes with those tame little
    tootsies
and dream about me — plead for me — [1]

This poem focuses our attention on the commonalities of needs and wants of many women as they grow older. They want everything "now" as they wanted "then." The woman in this poem, old and ill, close to death, still feels the strong pull of love and sex and the memory of her experiences. Both men and women can remain lovers through the ninth decade. Interest, activity, and real capacity persist in sex and sexuality in many older men and women. Significant to activity throughout the later years is the finding in survey research that sexually active lives in youth and middle years probably ensures sexual interest and energy maintenance in the older years (Pfeiffer & Davis, 1972).

There is a formidable history of the significance of sexuality in the story of the human family from primitive to modern times. Magic, strange elixers, potions, sorcery, folk medicine remedies, particular plant and animal tissues have all played a role, at one time or another, in the never-ending efforts to improve and maintain sexual "prowess." In its oft-repeated identification with youth and longevity, the maintenance of capacity for sexual expression has been perceived as a major part of a "life force" − even an important ally in the fight against death (Trimmer, 1970).

Sexual Expression: Anatomy/Physiology are not Separable from Behavioral and Environmental Dimensions

The expression of human sensuality, sexuality is a consequence of prenatal developmental and postnatal learning experiences. With the years, it becomes increasingly evident that the whole person − personality, physiology and the integrated life's experiences − is involved in sensual/ sexual behavior. Most persons are in possession of the biological capacity for reproduction and other physical, sexual activities. But it is apparent that human sexual expression is more than orgasm, more than the conception of the next generation, more than sex hormones and genitalia − connected in countless ways to all the aspects of living related to the reality of the two sexes.

Novelist John Fowles (1973) has said that to talk about the physiology of sex without the psychology, without societal influences, is like talking about all parts of a ship and not knowing how to steer it. It is equally misleading to raise psychosocial factors of sexual behavior without reference to the physiology. There is continual interaction among the physiology, the psyche, and society; e.g. a pain in the chest or abdomen may quickly abort the thought of lovemaking. Similarly, a positive, warm thought of someone you love and/or desire is quickly translated into changing hormonal levels. A recent study by *Psychology Today* (Gorney & Cox, 1973), reported the responses to questionnaires to determine how people feel about their sexuality. Out of more than 20,000 responses to 100 questions about sexual practices and attitudes, only 9% were from men and women over 45 years of age. One letter is particularly poignant and speaks to the intense physiological and affective needs of the middle and later years.

"I lost my first husband when I was forty-five years old, and the second one after only three weeks of a honeymoon at 48. What happens to such a woman as I, wanting sex, copulation, love, but wanting it only within the proper Victorian limits, yet feeling very wanton and very bad at times? There are nights and days and weeks and months with no opportunity to meet a man or men. This can be so eroding; it is sad and frightening. I am one who is starved beyond endurance." That it is a starvation seems clear, that it is a starvation for the expression of one's very identity is frequently ignored.

The Physiology

As with many other organ systems, the reproductive system of both men and women does change with time, becoming less efficient with age, especially as measured in terms of the potential for progeny. Most people accept the gradual decline in many other body functions — accommodating to the limits of efficiency and performance that can be expected with growing older. This is especially true if pathology is absent.

However, changes in the reproductive system are viewed with apprehension and fear. Even the most modest of dysfunctions conjures up the image of asexuality. Reproductive decline suggests the end of productive life. The culture still largely equates sexual performance with manliness and womanliness, with youth and vitality. Few changes with age are so threatening to ego, identity and the sense of well being, so suggestive of one's mortality and impending death. In view of these images and expectations of aging and the physical changes of the reproductive system, a conflict is created between human needs and an apparently inadequate capacity. The continuing human needs for intimacy, love, human interchange, and sense of self are coupled to the concern for failure as a sexually responsive person with or without a partner.

Impotence, sexual disinterest, and general dysfunction with age are specters which grow from the mythology of age as a whole. The overall images of aging as disease with consequent illness (even invalidism), as dependent and lonely; of declining learning and work capacities, decreasing sexual capacities; of critically limiting appropriate roles − all lower self esteem. Many older persons still accept this diminished image (along with other age groups) − and the observed reduced activity may in part be the fulfillment of that expectation. Constant repetition has reinforced the asexual "third sex" category, and large numbers of older persons and associated professions act accordingly.

The declining physiological efficiency of the reproductive function with age occurs gradually and involves primarily the neuromuscular and circulatory systems. There is little evidence that these physical changes are sufficient to account for the dramatic decrease or absence of sexual activity that the stereotype suggests. In both sexes, the time necessary to reach appropriate levels of excitement prior to orgasm is increased, the period (seconds) of orgasm is decreased. Nevertheless, the orgasmic experience remains as satisfying and pleasurable as ever. There are some overall physiological consequences common to men and women alike, generally conceded to be related to the decreasing male and female sex hormones. These changes include alterations in sleep patterns, weight gain, receding hair growth, loss of hair color, and the loss of genital tissue.

As with many other physiological parameters, changes in sexual anatomy, physiology, and behavior are variable in rate and appearance among the same age cohort − a reflection of the uniqueness of older persons. Not all the expected changes may occur within the same individual. The specifics of these changes in the male and female are helpful in understanding the changing nature of the sex act.

The male. While the identification of a "menopause" for men is not possible, there is growing agreement that a climacteric period of 10-20 years can be differentiated with examination over time. The sex hormones, particularly testosterone, decrease with age, the decline starting later (on the average) than in women. Older men have been known to father offspring even at 100 — which represents a considerable difference from the older female's capacity for childbearing, generally at an end with menopause. The lower levels of testosterone are accompanied by lowered rates of spermatogenesis, with fewer sperm, and fewer that are viable. Sex hormones are involved in the reproductive structure and function from conception through old age; they stimulate sexual attraction and libido (desire). These same hormones affect other developmental processes: protein synthesis, salt and water balance, bone growth and resorption, cardiovascular function, and possibly the capacity for immune surveillance.

Muscles begin to sag, testes are more flaccid, and the diameters of testicular tubules that store and carry sperm become increasingly narrowed by layers of non-productive cells. Generally, the prostate gland grows larger, its contractions weaker. These prostatic changes contribute to the reduction in the volume and viscosity of the seminal fluid with the resulting decrease in the force of the ejaculate.

As a sexual partner, the older male usually exhibits measurable differences in responsiveness and activity. Frequency of intercourse, intensity of sensation, speed of attaining erection, and the force of the ejaculation are all reduced. One aspect increases with age: unlike the older female, the late middle-aged and older male becomes aware of an increase in the refractory period — a longer recovery time is necessary before another erection can be achieved. There may be an interval of 12-24 hours before many normal men can redevelop penile erection (Masters & Johnson, 1970). If persistent illness or debilitating disease can be avoided, erectile ability is maintained. However, longer, more intense, and greater direct stimulation is necessary to achieve erection (Masters & Johnson, 1970; Oaks, Melchiode, & Ficher, 1976). The two-stage aspect of orgasm of the younger male is typically reduced to one: the first stage of ejaculatory inevitability becomes brief, eventually tends to disappear. The orgasmic period is shorter, and there is a rapid detumescence (loss of erection) after ejaculation. It is also increasingly apparent that the urgency and capacity for ejaculation at every sexual experience is reduced. Yet, once erection is achieved, it can be maintained for a longer period. **The female.** The climacteric for the woman may extend 20 years, from the mid-thirties to the mid-fifties and occasionally beyond. Recently, attempts to differentiate carefully between climacteric and menopause in the human female suggest the climacteric may be "a transitory phase in the human female between the ages of reproductive and non reproductive ability." Beyond the specific menopause which occurs during the climacteric, other clinical, metabolic, psychosocial, and crosscultural factors contribute to the complex picture (Utian, 1976). As with males, the physiological changes proceed gradually, slowly, and are considered complete with the final cessation of the menses and loss of fertility. The menopause, characterized by the loss of ovulation and therefore minimal potential for fertility, is associated with the end of menstrual bleeding and often accompanied by other body-wide changes.

Women in their middle years present different body contours: skin elasticity decreases everywhere in the body, the breasts sag, the abdominal skin is often wrinkled and scarred with purple stretch marks, the muscles of the limbs show increasing lack of muscle tone, and the "battle" of various bulges may be underway. Though fatty tissue slowly diminishes around the vulva, decreasing lean muscle mass with age is accompanied by an increased proportion of fat tissue in other parts of the body. Estrogen and progesterone continue their gradual, downward levels and activities, due in large part to the decreasing ovarian follicles. Decreased fertility, irregular and/or absent menses, blood vessel instability, slow atrophy of the genitalia generally proceed in that sequence. The degree and rate of these changes will vary with the highly individualized peri-menopausal pattern of each woman.

A number of subjective symptoms include a wide range that are not exclusive to the menopause/climacteric, but have been typically cited in an order of frequency: hot flashes (70%), sweating (54%), dizziness (46%), acute increase in blood pressure (66% of all woman 6 to 24 months postmenopausal) (Lauritzen, 1973). Palpitation, anxiety, nervousness, depression, headaches, loss of appetite, and insomnia appear less frequent and are probably not characteristic of menopause (Weg, 1976). However, equally represented in the research is the position that the majority of middle-aged and older women (more than 75%) move through the menopause with none or very few of the aforementioned. A most recent study of data from a multiphasic health screening program by the Pacific Health Research Institute of Hawaii on females of Caucasian and Japanese origin reported that about 75% of the sample reported no symptoms (Goodman, Stewart & Gilbert, 1977) as opposed to 26% of cases in a self-reported menopausal investigation (Crawford & Hooper, 1972).

Interesting studies have addressed the issue of cultural influence on the menopausal experience. Some societies reward women for having come to the end of their fertile period, and they experience few symptoms (Flint, 1976). Other cultures punish woman for having arrived at the close of her youth, her productive years (Van Keep, 1976). In the American society (many western societies), the still widespread emphasis on youth/beauty reflects the "punish" morality which conceivably can be implicated with a more severe symptomology of the menopause. Additional psychosocial factors have also been identified with the exacerbation or negation of associated menopausal symptoms. Women who have identified only with the roles of housewife and mother tend to have a more difficult (physically and psychologically) menopause/climacteric, whereas those who work or have additional purposive roles are aware of minimal or no difficulties (Neugarten, 1970; Neugarten & Datan, 1976; Bart, 1976).

Low levels of estrogenic hormones are maintained throughout the later years as a result of androgen synthesis by the adrenals. These androgens are converted to estrogen-like substances in various fat depots in the body. Nevertheless, with the years, the relative steroid starvation leads to a gradual atrophy of the uterus, vagina, and a reduction in size and firmness of related genital tissues. With some women, there may be a moderate regression of secondary sexual characteristics.

A loss of tissue leaves the mons and major labia less full. The vaginal mucosa thins, and the canal is somewhat shorter, the rugal pattern smoothing out. There may be occasional or frequent estrogen-deficient vaginitis. Glands which lubricate the vagina (Bartholin glands) decline in number and activity. Because of these changes, the vagina may become friable, crack and bleed. The closely related urinary organ system – urethra and bladder – may exhibit similar atrophy. Although the clitoris may be somewhat reduced in size, there is "no objective evidence to date to suggest any appreciable loss in sensate focus" (Masters & Johnson, 1970).

As an interested, responsive sexual partner, the older woman appears to be advantaged. "There is no time limit drawn by advancing years to female sexuality" (Masters & Johnson, 1966, p. 247). Multiorgasmic capacity remains, her physiology is more than adequate, her interest is high – but infrequent opportunity and an early Victorian sex education frustrate expression in the absence of a marriage partner. What has become clear as a result of the studies noted is that menopausal and postmenopausal women lose their fertility – but the libido remains intact! As with the male, the intensity of the physiological response to effective stimulation is reduced through all four phases of the sexual cycle (see Table II). Coitus may be less than satisfactory; painful for some postmenopausal women. Penetration by the penis (intromission) may be a problem for the thinning vagina, compounded by decreased lubrication. Under hormonal deprivation, the uterine contractions of orgasm which were rhythmic and smooth, become more spasmodic, irregular and fewer in number. Some women may experience a frequency of urination as well as burning sensations. Lubrication of the vulval and vaginal areas takes longer to achieve, the excitement level is slower to develop, the plateau stage lasts longer, and consequently orgasm takes more time to reach. Fortuitously, these facts are complementary to a similar state for the older male, who needs more time to achieve an erection but is able to maintain it longer. Older men and women would appear to have more time for the mutual pleasuring that can only enhance the sexual experience physically and emotionally.

Consequences of Illness and Disease:
Disinterest, Frustration, Dysfunction, Impotence

It is apparent that sensuality/sexuality are part of the whole person all through the lifespan and that the normal aging of the reproductive system leaves more than adequate capacity. What, then, accounts for the damaging non-feeling, impotent stereotype of the later years?

One prevailing view among lay persons and health professional alike considers aging as disease, rather than the existence of disease as an accompaniment to age. To be sure, some disease in the older years is a reality, but not inevitable − normal aging does exist (Weg, 1975). Among other resulting behaviors on the part of professionals and society at large, there is the noticeable imposition on older persons of the "sick role." Moreover, the number of chronic diseases which have so far resisted easy treatment and cure lends credence to the sick/invalid image. It is only a short path from the stereotype of a sick, dependent, almost frail person to "asexual." Ordinary human needs and wants can be denied more easily, and are. In so doing the elders are separated, not only by the years, but by the denial of participation in activities still considered the province of the young and the well. This reinforces the supposed significant difference between the aged and everyone else which can enable the rest of society to put out of sight and legitimate function the deep-seated fears of aging and death.

The other major source of the image of sexual disinterest and dysfunction does relate to the level of overall health and function: systemic diseases, excessive work patterns and related fatigue syndrome, excessive eating, alcoholism, drug abuse, disease and surgery of the urogenital system, and depression. Most of these factors could affect sexual interest and function at any age − though the incidence of depression, for example, does increase with age.

The increase in chronic disease, singly or in combination, includes hypertension, coronary disease, diabetes, arthritis, emphysema, and cancer. Of lesser prevalence but with comparable effects on desire and function are malnutrition, anemia, osteoporosis/osteomalacia. One of the underlying concerns in people who are sick is the fear that the stress of sexual involvement will aggravate the illness and possibly cause death (Masters & Johnson, 1970; Rubin, 1966 a,b.) This fear is unfounded; in most instances the heightened sense of well being, the improved circulation, and the shared pleasures not only have a generally salutory effect on health but more than outweigh the approximately 0.3% to less than 1% fatalities during intercourse that have been reported (Butler & Lewis 1973, 1976).

Potency (impotence) is a function of many variables: drug therapy, diabetes, stress, boredom, concern with career, other psychogenic factors, surgery of urogenital system. There are measurable differences between impotence of organic and psychogenic origin. Organic-based impotence finds onset slow, libido reduced, and an inability to masturbate or stimulate erection in any way. Psychogenic-based impotence finds onset abrupt; masturbation to orgasm ability is maintained, and the condition is frequently reversible.

Drug abuse

Widespread drug use and abuse among older persons may grow directly from the prevalent medical practice of palliation for any complaint or dysfunction among elders (Townsend, 1971; Lamy & Kitler, 1971; Kayne, 1976; Weg, 1973). Alcohol, marijuana and a large number of tranquilizers (e.g., chlorpromazine, Librium, Mellaril, Resperine) weaken erection and delay ejaculation; continued use may lead to impotency.

Laver (1974) in a study of Australian severely hypertensive males found that sexual activity is often absent or decreased. Loss of erectile ability, in the face of intact libido and sexual arousal, is the most frequent complaint with antihypertensive drug therapy. Especially important was the self reporting by patients — they appear certain that whatever the prescribed drugs they were using, the pills were the cause for any difficulty with their sexual potency. Since a large proportion of impotence before 80 or 90 is psychogenic in origin (Butler & Lewis, 1976), fear and expectation of impotence will frequently result in impotence.

Coronary disease

Only severe coronary pathology should result in abstinence. It was found that sexual activity was resumed on an average of 13.7 weeks after the coronary attack, but earlier with those who had been more active sexually prior to the attack (Hellerstein & Friedman, 1970). Although sexual intercourse of short duration has not been proven to be specifically beneficial to the circulation, it cannot be viewed as a threat to health, with its capacity to reduce physical and emotional tensions.

Diabetes

Despite continued libido, many diabetic men and women do experience sexual dysfunction. Women report difficulty in vaginal lubrication, although adequate estrogen is present. A number of factors may be involved: neuropathy, susceptibility to infection, microvascular changes, and the chronicity of the diabetes (Kolodny, 1971). Kolodny, Kahn, Goldstein, & Barnett (1974) report that a number of investigators indicate that as many as 50% of diabetic males with organic impotence are unable to masturbate or stimulate erection in any way. Although some studies have suggested that low testosterone may be responsible, frequently concentration is within normal limits. Hormone therapy has not been successful in treating diabetes-related impotence (Kolodny, et al., 1974). Recent evidence has emphasized a neurological basis for the diabetes-associated impotence. Polsters (small valve-like structures) containing smooth muscle, near the *corpora cavernosa,* are under control of the autonomic nervous system. Any difficulty with neural transmission may interfere with increased blood flow to the erectile tissues (Weiss, 1972). Retrograde ejaculation and premature ejaculation may also be part of the complex picture of sexual function of the diabetic.

Osteoporosis

This disease is a painful disorder which presents a loss of total bone mass that results in fragile bones, difficulty in maintaining posture, and frequent acute pain. At one time, osteoporosis was considered primarily estrogen-dependent, postmenopausal pathology. Although the incidence in women is four times that in men, treatment with estrogen does not benefit everyone (Bartter, 1973). The current treatment of choice includes increased dietary calcium, estrogen, and fluoride (Jowsey, 1976).

Surgery — Urogenital System

Large numbers of older men and women have ended their sexual activity upon the advent of pelvic surgery. However, clinical data suggest that in spite of the apparent depression of desire and capacity for climax after prostatectomies and hysterectomies, there is no physiological inevitability of such consequences (Finkle & Moyers, 1960). In one investigation by Patterson and Craig (1963) they found 80% of patients following a prostatectomy and 70% of women following hysterectomy retain potency. However, the type of prostate surgery is central to maintenance of potency: in a number of investigations suprapubic and ansurethal surgery among 94 individuals left 80% with no significant change in sexual potency; 69% of 61-70 year olds retained potency one year after surgery, independent of age. However, perineal exposure and removal of prostate results in a loss of potency (Gold & Hotchkiss, 1969) and coital enjoyment. Retrograde ejaculation was frequent as well.

What to Do: Make the Most of Capacity

1. **Hormone Replacement Therapy**
   Since some of the apparent disinterest and cessation of function in the older female may be related to tissues that are less responsive, difficulty with lubrication and intercourse due to steroid starvation, serious consideration of replacement should be undertaken. Only hormone replacement can effectively alleviate some of the physiological symptomology — vasomotor instability, vaginitis, and inadequate lubrication (Masters & Johnson; 1970, Schleyer-Saunders, 1971). Since the report by Ziel and Finkle (1975) of their examination of data from four different studies indicated the increased risk of endometrial cancer among users of conjugated estrogen, caution and individual evaluation

must be exercised. It is therefore, more important than ever before to test the efficacy of combined estrogen and progesterone replacement. Dr. Marilyn Pratt (medical practitioner in Los Angeles) has used this approach for 16 years with excellent, safe results for her patients. Other physicians, Greenblatt (1977), Jern (1973), and Nachtigall (1976) have also been successful in long term use (30 yrs., 16 yrs., over 10 yrs. respectively) of this procedure. Such sequential therapy would appear to minimize the effect of estrogen in the stimulation of proliferation of the uterine wall.

Hormone (testosterone) replacement therapy for men with impotent experiences is not generally considered to be clearly effective. Fellman (1975) believes that the improvement in erective ability is not a direct result of the androgen but relates to "(1) a sense of well being associated with anabolic androgenic substances, (2) the physician's confidence that this is a problem amenable to treatment, and (3) the allaying of anxiety during the course of treatment." More work is needed to pursue the details of impotence in older males and the disadvantages as well as advantages of androgen therapy.

2. **Sexual Therapy Wherever Necessary**
    If there is the acceptance of lifelong sexuality as the norm, then elders as well as youth deserve help in a form that is acceptable and useful. Masters and Johnson (1970) report a 50% success rate with older clients at the Reproductive Biology Research Foundation in St. Louis. They estimate that the success rate would be greater if the problem had not existed for a long time. Dr. Mary Ann Sviland in her therapeutic approach attempts to achieve "sexual liberation" for the older couples with whom she works. Details of her approach can be found in Chapter 8 of this book.

3. **Sexual Education All Through the Lifespan**
    The middle and later years are years in which the personality continues to grow and the changing realities of life call for new information and practices. Since sexual behavior is learned, information could make a difference in beliefs and practices. Knowledge about the

facts of lifespan changes in sexuality could prevent anxiety, fear, and minimize risk to an already troubled ego. Information could provide the confidence to explore ways to remain sexually involved commensurate with each individual's lifestyle. Allied health professions have a responsibility to insure adequate consultation and education for older persons concerning potential consequences for sexual activity of urogenital surgery, coronary disease, diabetes, hypertension, and any other systemic disturbance.

For many without available partners, particular discussion of the role of masturbation may make possible another way for older persons to know and enjoy their bodies. Many sex therapists suggest that masturbation may be useful in maintaining potency in men and lubrication in women. Moreover, masturbation "releases tensions, stimulates sexual appetite, contributing to well being" (Weg, 1975b).

4. Research Goals
    To undertake careful testing of old and new hypertensive drugs

    To consider all side effects, especially those related to potency

    To undertake studies that would elucidate the aging mechanisms

    To identify factors which provide women with an 8 year advantage over men in life expectancy; to identify factors that would increase the life span and vigor of men, which would enable partners to stay together longer

    To undertake a major effort into the etiology, prevention, and appropriate treatment (rather than palliation) of chronic diseases which currently affect the lives of so many in the later years

5. **To Alter Attitudes Toward Aging, Toward the Needs of Elders, Toward Men and Women**
    To equalize sex roles, provide women and men with equal opportunities and recognition

To encourage dating and marriage of younger men with older women

To develop a greater understanding, constructive attitudes concerning homosexuality, polygamy

6. **To Encourage Oldsters to Enjoy Each Other**
   To be released from the tradition and time-bound practice of sex "only in the dark, at night;" to engage in sex play and intercourse at period of maximum energy — in the morning

7. **To Accept the Reality of Individual Differences Among Older Persons in the Variability of Sexual Expression**

8. **To Insure that the Helping Professions See the Old as Persons**
   Appropriate education about aging and the later years is necessary to carry out their responsibilities

   It is therefore the responsibility of those professions (medicine, nursing, social work, etc.) to alter the curricula and requirements in keeping with the changes in population

Closing Thoughts

The most destructive reality for the sexuality of older persons is related, not to the gradual, relatively small changes in human sexual performance, but rather to the mythology of impotence and disinterest that is part of the overall negative image of aging. Equally destructive is the suggestion that all older persons must be sexually active and expressive. Some suffer the alienation of aloneness; others have given up (at times, in defense) sexual interests. A new norm, a new conformity which demands that all elders must be sexually involved, is as stereotypic as the old sexless myth.

Evidence is overwhelming that the need for intimate, affective relationships exists for most men and women all through life. Contrary to the mythical "neuter, non-person" assignation for those who have grown old, older men and women are capable of fulfilling a part of those needs in sensual and sexual expression. It may even be that the need and the pleasure in its satisfaction may be greater in the later years than in youth, since the busy variety of life's ambience (in people and happenings) has diminished or disappeared. The touching warmth and caring shared with another will strengthen a tenuous self image, reinforce or restore a sense of well being, and celebrate feeling alive.

It is my hope that the research in sexuality will move beyond quantitation (the number of orgasms per week) to the quality of the relationship for the whole person. In so doing, we may come to see more concern with affection, with desire, and with the part played by the physical aspect of love and intercourse. Intercourse and orgasm without affection become less meaningful with the years. The recent emphases on the "mechanics" of genital response appears to depersonalize the interaction and may disadvantage the oldster who does not seek the goal of "excellent technique."

In a climate of awareness and concern for human needs and wants, we shall see an important move away from the goal-oriented passion of youth to the person-oriented intimacy of the mature and later years.

References

Bart, P. Depression in middle aged women. In S. Cox, *Female psychology: The emerging self.* Chicago: Science Research Associates, 1976.

Bartter, F. C. Bone as a target organ: Toward a better definition of testosterone. *Perspectives in Biology and Medicine,* 1973, *16,* 215-231.

Butler, R. N., & Lewis, M. I. *Aging and mental health.* St. Louis: C. V. Bosby, 1973.

Butler, R. N., & Lewis, M. I. *Sex after sixty.* New York: Harper & Row. 1976.

Crawford, M. P., & Hooper, D. Menopause, aging, and family. *Social Science and Medicine,* 1973, *7,* 469-482.

Fellman, S. L. Should androgens be used to treat impotence in men over 50? *Medical Aspects of Human Sexuality,* 1975, *9*(7), July 1975, 32-43.

Finkle, A., & Moyers, T. Sexual potency in aging males: IV. Status of private patients before and after prostatectomy. *Journal of Urology,* 1960, *84,* 152-157.

Flint, M. Cross-cultural factors that affect age of menopause. In P. A. Van Keep, R. B. Greenblatt, & M. Albeaux-Fernet (Eds.), *Consensus on menopause research.* Baltimore: University Park Press, 1976.

Fowles, J. In S. Gorney & C. Cox, *After forty*. New York: Dial Press, 1973.

Gold, F. & Hotchkiss, R. Sexual potency following simple prostatectomy. *New York State Journal of Medicine*, 1969, *69*, 2987.

Goodman, M., Stewart, C. J., & Gilbert, F. Patterns of menopause. *Journal of Gerontology*, 1977, *32*(3), 291-298.

Gorney, S., & Cox, C. *After forty*. New York: Dial Press, 1973.

Greenblatt, R. Estrogens in cancer change the way you treat postmenopausal patients. *Modern Medicine*, March 1977, 47-48.

Hellerstein, H. E. Heart disease and sex. *Medical Aspects of Human Sexuality*, 1971, *5*(6), June 1971, 24-35.

Hellerstein, H. E., & Friedman, E. H. Sexual activity and the post coronary patient. *Scandinavian Journal of Rehabilitation Medicine, 1970, 125*, 987; *Medical Aspects of Human Sexuality*, 1979, *3*, 70.

Jern, H. Z. *Hormone therapy of menopause and aging*. Springfield, Illinois: Charles C. Thomas, 1973.

Jowsey, J. Prevention and treatment of osteoporosis. In M. Winick (Ed.), *Nutrition and aging*. New York: John Wiley & Sons, 1976.

Kayne, R. C. Drugs and the aged. In I. M. Burnside (Ed.), *Nursing and the aged*. New York: McGraw-Hill, 1976.

Kolodny, R. C. Sexual dysfunction in diabetic females. *Diabetes,* 1971, *20, 557.*

Kolodny, R. C., Kahn, C., Goldstein, H., & Barnett, D. Sexual dysfunction in diabetic men. *Diabetes, 1974, 23,* 306-309.

Lamy, P., & Kitler, M. Drugs and the geriatric patient. *Journal of the American Geriatrics Society, 1971, 19*(1), 23-33.

Lauritzen, C. The management of the premenopausal and the postmenopausal patient. *Frontiers of Hormone Research, 1973, 2*(2), 21.

Laver, M. C. Sexual behavior patterns in male hypertensives. *Australian, New Zealand Journal of Medicine, 1974, 4,* 29-31.

Masters, W. H., & Johnson, V. E. *Human sexual inadequacy*. Boston: Little, Brown, 1970.

Masters, W. H., & Johnson, V. E. *Human sexual response*. Boston: Little, Brown, 1966.

Merriam, E. *A conversation against death*. (Poem.) *Ms Magazine*, September 1972, 80-83.

Nachtigall, L. Behind the estrogen-cancer headline. *Medical World News, 1976, 17,* 39.

Neugarten, B. L. Dynamics of transition of middle age to old age: Adaptation and the life cycle. *Journal of Geriatric Psychiatry*, 1970, *4,* 71-87.

Neugarten, B. L., & Datan, N. The middle years. *Journal of Geriatric Psychiatry, 1976, 9*(1), 41-59.

Oaks, W. W., Melchiode, G. A., & Ficher, I. (Eds.). *Sex and the life cycle.* San Francisco: Grune & Stratton, 1976.

Pfeiffer, E., & Davis, G. C. Determinants of sexual behavior in the elderly. *Journal of the American Geriatric Society,* 1972, *20*(4), 151-158.

Pratt, M. Personal communication, October 1977.

Rubin, I. Common sex myths. *Sexology,* 1966a, *32,* 512-514.

Rubin, I. Sex after 40 and after 70. In R. Brecher & E. Brecher (Eds.), *An analysis of human sexual responses.* New York: New American Library, Inc., 1966b.

Schleyer-Saunders, E. Results of hormone implants in the treatment of the climateric. *Journal of the American Geriatrics Society,* 1971, *19*(2), 114-121.

Townsend, C. *Old age: The last segregation.* New York: Grossman, 1971.

Utian, W. H. The climacteric syndrome: A workshop report. In P. A. Van Keep, R. B. Greenblatt, & M. Albeaux-Fernet (Eds.), *Consensus on menopause research.* Baltimore: University Park Press, 1976.

Van Keep, P. A. Psychosocial aspects of the climacteric. In P. A. Van Keep, R. B. Greenblatt, & M. Albeaux-Fernet (Eds.), *Consensus on menopause research.* Baltimore: University Park Press, 1976.

Weg, R. B. Changing physiology of aging: Normal and pathological. In D. S. Woodruff & J. E. Birren (Eds.), *Aging: Scientific perspectives and social issues.* New York: Van Nostrand, 1975a.

Weg, R. B. Drug interaction with the changing physiology of the aged: Practice and potential. In Ronald C. Kayne (Ed.), *Drugs and the elderly.* Los Angeles: Andrus Gerontology Center, University of Southern California, 1978.

Weg, R. B. Normal aging changes in the reproductive system. In I. M. Burnside (Ed.), *Nursing and the aged.* New York: McGraw-Hill, 1976.

Weg, R. B. Sexual inadequacy in the elderly. In R. Goldman & M. Rockstein (Eds.), *The physiology and pathology of human aging.* New York: Academic Press, 1975b.

Weiss, H. D. The physiology of human penile erection. *Annals of Internal Medicine,* 1972, *76,* 793-799.

Ziel, H. K., & Finkle, W. D. Increased risk of endometrial carcinoma among users of conjugated estrogens. *New England Journal of Medicine,* 1975, *293*(23), 1167-70.

Footnotes

[1] From "A Conversation Against Death," a poem by Eve Merriam which was first published in *Ms Magazine,* September 1972, pp. 80-83. Reprinted by Permission of Eve Merriam, c/o International Creative Management.©1968 by Eve Merriam.

Sexuality and Aging: An Internist's Perspective

6

Isadore Rossman

Up until very recently, the physician in practice was in the disquieting position of having to prescribe on the basis of opinions regarding aging and sexuality, rather than a body of data and facts. But we are still very far from being certain as to whether some sexual behaviors or deficits should be regarded as falling within normal limits. Nor do we know, for some age groups, what should be regarded as reversible or responsive to treatment or irreversible and best left untreated. The American Psychiatric Association not long ago reversed itself on the question of whether or not homosexuality should be called a disease, to cite an unrelated instance of the controversy over what is pathologic and what is not. There are equally vague areas in relation to the effect of aging on sexuality.

There are many practical and therapeutic aspects to the problem which can perhaps be highlighted by citing a clinical example. A not uncommon one is that of the male patient who appears in the doctor's office at age 60 complaining of a marked diminution if not a virtually complete loss of sexual capacity. The differential diagnosis of this complaint ranges far and wide. If one is a strong believer in what has been termed "the male menopause," then this is the first major possibility that comes to mind. One might think of ordering tests for blood and urinary testosterone levels, and perhaps an evaluation of pituitary activity such as the urinary gonadotropin. If borderline results are turned up, a trial of testosterone therapy may be ushered in. Or, the patient may be referred to an endocrinologist who may also have a strong personal belief in the existence of a male menopause on the basis of just such kinds of referrals. With a brisk referral practice of this sort, the endocrinologist may well conclude that the male menopause is a common phenomenon, and publish papers to that effect.

If the internist who is consulted happens to be a diabetologist, his first free association (which is all that differential diagnosis is) may be to diabetes. Diabetes enjoys an undue reputation as a cause of impotence in males so the first test might be a glucose tolerance test. Or if the internist happens to have a psychosomatic bent, he may regard such a complaint as highly likely to be psychogenic, and think first of instituting psychiatric consultation or psychotherapy. The nature of medical practice and the complexity of our patients are such that any of these approaches may uncover some promising diagnostic material. Blood testosterone levels may be borderline. Glucose tolerance tests may show a one hour level in excess of 180 and a two hour level in excess of 120 mg %. One of the effects of aging is the development of glucose intolerance; determinations which signify diabetes in the young or middle-aged probably do not for those in older age groups. Finally, a psychiatric evaluation, the nature of our society and times being what they are, may well reveal a patient in middle age somewhat depressed over his life history and his prospects, and perhaps not completely happy with all aspects of his marital life. Thus it may be clear to the psychiatrically oriented internist that there are aspects of anxiety and depression in the patient's presenting complaint. The problem is not resolved despite all of these positive facts and consultations. Rather, both internist and patient may face difficult times. More testosterone, less depression, with some improvement in glucose tolerance seem to be indicated.

However, still another possibility exists, which is that the patient is normal albeit hypofunctioning. With biologic variables, it is not always easy to distinguish between normal and abnormal; sometimes our limited knowledge leads us to consider the normal abnormal. An example from an area in which I once did research concerns the changes that occur in the lining of the uterus after ovulation. Edema develops between the cells of the stroma as does infiltration with lymphocytes and other cells. Increased serration of the glands follows with tortuosity and congestion of the blood vessels. This microscopic picture, on the basis of studies derived from other organs, was regarded as an inflammatory process, and was called endometritis. It was not until 1907 that Hitschmann and Adler showed that "endometritis glandularis" was a classificational delusion. All of the "pathologic" findings were perfectly normal progesterone-induced cyclic changes; indeed, they were proof of ovulation.

Declining sexual capacity with age has long been a theme in novels, plays, operas, and jokes. It remained for Kinsey, Pomeroy, and Martin (1948) to document the fact that sexual activity reaches a peak in the 20's and declines steadily decade after decade thereafter. A 2% rate of impotency at age 40 increased to 18% by 60, 25% by 65, 55% by 75, and 75% by 80. Kinsey's figures were regarded with some suspicion because of the fact that they were elicited in interviews with volunteers. However, Finkel (1971) found a 31% incidence of impotence in the 55-59 group, rising to 75% at 75, as did Bowers, Cross, and Lloyd (1963); both worked with urological patients. Newman and Nichols (1960), as part of the Duke Longitudinal Study, reported that more than 40% of married subjects between 60 and 70 were no longer having sexual relations, and there was an abrupt fall off at 75 and over, with only about a quarter of the married subjects still having sexual relations. In a more elaborate analysis of the same patient population by Verwoerdt, Pfeiffer and Wang (1969), declining activity, not necessarily paralleled by declining interest, was again noted. In both of these studies a lucky residue of elderly subjects was found able to continue sexual relations into extreme old age, albeit with diminishing frequency.

In a recent report concerning a patient population of 2,801 males in a private urological practice (Pearlman, 1972), roughly 80% in the 30-39 age group, 68% in the 40-49 group, 50% in their 50's, 25% in their 60's, and 10% in their 70's had intercourse at least once a week. Eleven percent of the males between 50-59 reported no intercourse; this rose to 36% in the 60-69 group, and 59% in the 70-79 group (Table I).

Table I
Incidence of Impotence
Cited by Various
Authors*

AGE	% IMPOTENCE	AGE	% IMPOTENCE
Kinsey		**Bowers**	
40	1.9	60-64	28.0
45	2.6	65-69	50.0
50	6.7	70-74	61.0
55	6.7		
60	18.4	**Newman**	
65	25.0		
70	27.0	60-64	40.0
75	55.0	65-69	37.0
80	75.0	70-74	42.0
		75+	75.0
Finkle			
55-59	31.0	**Perlman, Kobashi**	
60-64	37.0	40-49	5.0
65-69	37.0	50-59	11.3
70-74	61.0	60-69	36.6
75-79	76.0	70-79	59.0
80+	60.0	80+	85.0

Figures from a socio-cultural background other than the American one are supplied by Cendron and Vallery-Masson from the Claude Bernard Center for Gerontology in Paris. The group studied was composed of consultants to the Center, a superior socio-economic and cultural group, and for the most part married. The sexual activity of different ages is as follows:

Table II*

Age Group	25	40	55-65	65-75
Median Age	25	40	59.9	68.5
Number	85	85	49	45

Median frequency of
    intercourse per month ± error factor

	27.6±3.1	17.2±1.8	3.9±0.7	1.8±0.3
Extreme Values	1-180	1-135	0-24	0-8

Particularly to be noted is the marked fall-off in frequency of sexual relations quite obviously manifest before age 40, with a steep decline in the 6th and 7th decades. Almost half the men at age 60 were no longer sexually potent. Both in the French study and in others, wide individual variations are noteworthy. Nonetheless, it remains a fact in all of the investigations that a marked falling off of sexual capacity occurs with age in the males, and a rising incidence of impotency past the 50-60 age period is indubitable. It is important to keep these facts in mind. In geriatric sexuality, we seem recently to be experiencing a revolution of rising expectations, if a possible pun may be forgiven. There seems to be a growing and increasingly widespread belief that with appropriate therapy, all older people are going to have more capability in sexual performance.

---

*From "The Effects of Age on Male Sexual Activity" by H. Cendron and J. Vallery-Masson, *La Presse Medicale*, 1970, *78*, 1795. MASSON, S. A. Paris.

There is no functional parameter of aging that falls off more steeply than sexual performance. Nevertheless, there seems to be a tendency to classify very old males who are still performing as an achievable norm rather than as unusual examples of sexual robustness. Perhaps it would be more in accord with the facts to regard them as obsessive, unable to give up a sex habit, and unlike the rest of their contemporaries. We have few if any clues as to why sexuality persists in some men into their 80's and disappears in other men in their 50's. It is certainly not related to broad questions of physical health, smoking, presence of chronic disease, alcoholism and drug ingestion or other factors which are known to sometimes impair sexual performance. Masters and Johnson (1970) in their therapeutic approach have placed a great deal of emphasis on the fear of failure, and shown that secondary impotence is reversible in some instances by a form of pleasant sexual and behavioral conditioning. It hardly seems likely that this can apply in total to the large population of males experiencing the typical diminution of sexual capabilities past the age of 50.

The extraordinary fall-off of sexual performance from the 20's to the 50's is not related to secretion of male hormones. Nor can other disorders which show an age-related increase, such as the rising incidence of diabetes or arteriosclerosis, be causative. One should not necessarily assume that psychological factors are regularly involved. The patient must be evaluated in relation to the statistical findings which indicate that his deficiency may not be as abnormal as has been claimed. In short, a 50-60 year old male complaining of diminished sexual desire or loss of potency may not be suffering from any readily identifiable disease process, whether physical or psychiatric. This does not imply that he may not be coaxed or stimulated into better sexual performance by appropriate circumstances, such as a seductive surrogate. Indeed, the most reliable treatment approach for such secondary impotence is currently the therapy described by Masters and Johnson (1970). Even when this is successful, the limits inherent in the patient's age group will still be apparent.

Male Menopause. There are, occasionally, clinical examples of middle-aged men complaining of loss of libido and potency, of hot flushes and sweats, who have low testosterone titers in their blood and who respond to testosterone injection. There is a great deal of question how common this phenomenon is. Selective series of cases emanating from consulting endocrinologists tell us nothing about statistical incidence. Blood testosterone studies of men in average physical health reveal no change in the assays throughout the 40's and 50's, and often little diminution in the 60's. The studies firmly establish the fact that there is no relationship between declining sexual capacity during these decades and hormone levels. Studies of pituitary activity such as insulin stimulation reveal no defect in aging males. Differential diagnosis is made much murkier by the fact that large numbers of males complaining of loss of potency are clinically depressed and loss of libido is a classical finding in depression. We happen to be living in a society at a time which is not conducive to good mental health. The rules are rigged in such a manner that they guarantee a high incidence of failure in the competitive life game. By the 6th decade of life, many males have found out they are not as successful as they had hoped to be and that their previously-held definitions of success are emptier than they had anticipated. In addition, boredom with life patterns and even marital patterns make it easy to perceive how this middle-aged depression could masquerade as "male menopause." To further complicate the matter of making a diagnosis, it is well established that blood testosterone levels may be significantly decreased by states of tension or depression. One must be careful in interpreting even a clinical trial. A mildly depressed, somewhat suggestible male, assured by an authoritative doctor that a shot in the arm will fix him, may well show an apparent response to a testosterone injection. The monkey gland transplants of the 20's illustrated this clearly. Such a clinical trial is no more persuasive in proving the existence of an endocrinopathy than would administration of a thyroid preparation leading to increased energy or pep demonstrate a pre-existing hypothyroid state. Thus, since there is no reliable relationship between aging and diminished blood testosterone levels, the administration of testosterone to older males is generally a fruitless way of restoring youthful sexual pep.

Coronary Artery Disease. Years ago the hapless victim of a myocardial infarction was treated in such a manner as to insure physical and psychiatric inadequacy when his six weeks in the hospital were over. He was allowed out of bed only after some weeks and with great tentativeness. The coronary care program the patient received at that time was correctly interpreted by him as indicating that he was in jeopardy. It was apparent that he had to be careful not to do anything that would accelerate the heart rate, and when, in his weakened condition, he was finally allowed to ambulate or perhaps totter, he was likely to find that small efforts would produce considerable tachycardia, and that he did truly suffer from considerable weakness. Many patients were convinced that either their days or their number of cardiac beats were numbered, and drew the appropriate, apparently prudent conclusion that they should limit their activity to a point which would draw the least on the limited cardiac reserve. In this context it is not at all surprising that many of them gave up sexual activity, a point of view regarded as not unreasonable by attending physicians of those days.

Needless to say, attitudes have undergone a complete reversal, in much the same manner as occured with the prolonged bed rest of the postpartum regimes of those days. Now, with the exception of patients who are left with severe myocardial insufficiency or congestive failure, we encourage all patients to resume as nearly normal life as they can. A number of studies have shown that the cardiac expenditure in intercourse is approximately that involved in climbing two flights of stairs. Hence if a post-coronary patient can climb two flights of stairs without significant or disabling symptomatology, there is no reason for forbidding sexual activity. Even patients who experience some angina in sexual circumstances find that prophylactic nitroglycerine may solve the problem.

Diabetes. Diabetes is often cited as a disorder which may produce loss of sexual functioning in the male, to such an extent that some have advocated routine glucose tolerance tests on men complaining of a recent onset of impotence. Poorly regulated diabetes is notorious for interfering with nerve cell functioning. Not only are the peripheral nerves often involved in diabetic neuropathic processes but also various of the cranial nerves (III, IV, VI, VII) are often impaired, along with nerves of the autonomic nervous system. Control of the diabetes, perhaps with an increased vitamin intake, has a favorable effect on some cases of diabetic impotence. But there is again a problem of differential diagnosis. We are faced with the question of whether the middle-aged man with a potency problem in whom chemical diabetes is also discovered is suffering from only one disorder or from two unrelated ones. If other signs of neuropathy are demonstrable, or if bladder function studies demonstrate neurogenic impairment, one might then conclude that such impotence in the diabetic is also of a neuropathic basis.

Alcoholism. Chronic alcoholism impairs potency as that great observer, Shakespeare, noted. One mechanism by which this may occur in males is through the impairment of hepatic function so that endogenous estrogens are not properly conjugated and metabolized. This may occur in association with Frank Laennec's cirrhosis in which gynecomastia and other evidences of femininization may be noted.

Hypothyroidism. A slowly progressive, often rather insidious, form of hypothyroidism can develop in the middle and late years. It produces slowing of cerebration and reactivity, puffiness, diminished energy and libido. Thyroid replacement therapy is curative. Unfortunately, too often there is sufficient associated atherosclerotic heart disease, attributed to the hypercholesterolemia; in such instances substitution therapy may bring on angina and is fraught with risks of sudden death. Encouragement of sexual performance is not a high priority goal in these clinicial circumstances, but improvement is certainly feasible and has been reported.

Hypopituitarism. Hypopituitarism produces a similar clinical picture with findings of adrenal insufficiency added thereto. Again, replacement therapy is fraught with perils, with adrenal crisis an added hazard. Many of the cases seen over recent decades were iatrogenic, the pituitary destruction man-made in an effort to control diabetic retinopathy or metastatic cancer. These associated disorders are as likely to wreck sexual performance as the ablative procedures, not to mention the depression likely to be present.

Tobacco and Other Drugs. Though a little tranquility may be desirable for sexual performance, full doses of drugs on some tranquilizing regimes may impair libido. The barbiturates and phenothiazines are common examples. This undesirable aspect of drugs apparently may be extended even to heavy cigarette consumption as has been pointed out in a number of studies, including the one by Cendron and Vallery-Masson (1975) cited earlier. Some heavy smokers when they quit note improved general health as well as improved libido. Documentation of the impact on sexual performance of other diseases is quite fragmented. Strokes may have a catastrophic impact on sexual performance, completely abolishing it. Most chronic diseases impair performance also, though for many years pulmonary tuberculosis enjoyed the opposite reputation. Critical evaluation of the allegations regarding pulmonary tuberculosis reveal that at least in the prechemotherapy days, many of the individuals suffering from this disorder were young and were kept at bed rest for months; that there would be some expression of libido in young persons kept in bed for long periods of time would hardly be unexpected.

Female Issues

Most reports in this field have dealt with male sexuality and aging. There has been a comparative neglect of that even larger group in the aging population, women. It would appear from the studies of Masters and Johnson (1966) that there is no loss of orgastic responsiveness in the older woman. The Duke Longitudinal Study also indicates that the sexual activity of the aging female can be related quite directly to the sexual activity of her mate. Whether this will hold for the new generation of liberated women, raised with far less inhibitions on birth control pills, remains to be seen. Both widowhood as well as widowerhood, are thus likely to lead to marked diminution in sexual functioning.

From the clinician's point of view the major therapeutic question is that of giving hormones to the post-menopausal woman. In the absence of such treatment, atrophic processes take over in the female reproductive tract, with shrinkage of the labia, narrowing and increasing dryness of the vagina, a decreasing capacity for lubrication, and certainly with some women, diminution of libido and capacity to respond pleasureably to sex. However, physicians have reversed former policies of giving estrogens on a more or less continuing basis because of the reported increase in endometrial cancer apparent after five or more years of estrogen administration. The topical administration of estrogenic creams may be reasonably safe and of value where regression postmenopausally produces pain.

Concluding Remarks

It remains a curious fact that during REM sleep, males experience erection, and this occurs in regular cycles throughout the night. The same males when awake may be unable to perform the sex act. There has been no satisfactory explanation for this discrepancy. However, Fisher (1966) at Mt. Sinai Hospital in New York has demonstrated that in old men REM erections are less full than in younger ones. Again we note a biologic relation between aging and a decreasing sexual reactivity. The marked downward slope of the curve for male sexuality with age may, like the decline in ovulation in women in their 40's followed by cessation of cycles, be an expression of Nature's intent not to have older human beings become parents. Granting that is so, sex activity as an interpersonal communication, as a manifestation of affection, and as an experience with overtones of youth, continue and have the more dominant meanings in middle and late life. It is the internist's role to encourage this and to provide it by any biologic or psychologic mechanism at his command.

References

Bowers, L. M., Cross, R. N., Jr., & Lloyd, F. A. Sexual function and urologic disease in the elderly male. *Journal of the American Geriatrics Society,* 1963, *11,* 647-652.

Cendron, Vallery-Masson. The effects of age on male sexual activity. *La Presse Medicale,* 1970, *78,* 1975.

Finkle, A. Sexual function during advancing age. In I. Rossman (Ed.), *Clinical geriatrics.* Philadelphia: J. B. Lippincott, 1971.

Fisher, C. Dreaming and sexuality. In R. M. Lowenstein, L. M. Newman, M. Schur, & A. J. Solnit (Eds.), *Psychoanalysis: A general psychology.* New York: International Universities Press, 1966.

Kinsey, A. C., Pomeroy, W. B., & Martin, C. I. *Sexual behavior in the human male.* Philadelphia: W. B. Saunders, 1948.

Masters, W. H., & Johnson, V. E. *Human sexual inadequacy.* Boston: Little, Brown, 1970.

Masters, W. H., & Johnson, V. E. *Human sexual response.* Boston: Little, Brown, 1966.

Newman, G., & Nichols, C. R. Sexual activities and attitudes in older persons. *Journal of the American Medical Association,* 1960, *173,* 33-35.

Pearlman, C. K. Frequency of intercourse in males at different ages. *Medical Aspects of Human Sexuality,* 1972, *6,* 92.

Verwoerdt, A., Pfeiffer, E., & Wang, H. Sexual behavior in senescence: Patterns of sexual activity and interest. *Geriatrics,* 1969, *24,* 137-154.

Sexual Problems in the Senior World 7

Alexander P. Runciman

It has been said that we spend the first half of our lives learning how to live and the last half trying to. Young people growing up today learn more about living and personal health before they are out of their teens than their parents did by middle age. Today's grandparents, people in their 60's and 70's—what did they know at sixteen?

The social milieu in which today's elderly grew to adulthood could hardly be said to have existed in today's era of enlightment. Burdened with superstitions, Puritan mores, and the Victorian syndrome, the most sophisticated knew little of the "facts of life." Even those few hardy pioneers who dared to turn on a light here and there were more often than not submerged in the abysmal ignorance of the period.

Thus, it was not a healthy climate for rational exploration of sexual problems; indeed, it was a time particularly insalubrious for sex exposure. Any idea that might shed a little light on the mystery of sex was discouraged. And so it remained a mystery—a mystery that was only a little changed from ancient legends to modern facts. It was certainly no time like the present. No wonder those who have lived from that period to the present are often shocked when confronted with the truths about sex. Their surprise, though pathetic, should be no surprise to the therapist. They have suffered too long under the erroneous concepts of the past to accept without some perplexity the initial questions of the therapist.

That is why counseling older people is often an exciting experience for the therapist. The elderly very often come to counseling with an openness and a new spirit of adventure which is valuable. They want to know what is new in research. When they discover some of the facts that have been established in sexual research, they eagerly make this information part of their lives.

It is a distinct pleasure to work with such people because they have seen enough of life to realize that some of the things that were originally presented to them as factual and doctrinal were not true. There is often a sense of humor that comes with the years, a humor about oneself and about life which is excellent conditioning for counseling. For many of the elderly, the sexual revolution has come about fifty years too late; they hear and read about it, but they cannot really be a part of it. Some still are weighted down with the idea that sex is not and never was an important part of their lives. Unless they were born neuter, such thinking is unfortunate and unfair to themselves.

That is why our present culture reflects an era of contradictions in the realm of sexuality. On the one extreme there is the period of youth where sex is accepted, encouraged, and exploited, but in middle and old age Victorian secrecy still shrouds sexual activity and interest. For older persons, it is an uncomfortable topic, the pervasive attitude being that it is just too embarrassing to have any place in open communication.

In the United States, the youth-oriented society sets the pace and the standards in sex. Who, for instance, could ever imagine a sexy-looking woman of fifty-five dressed in a negligee appearing enticingly on the pages of a fashion magazine? When have we seen a distinguished man of sixty dancing cheek to cheek with a gorgeous brunette of fifty-eight in a television commercial? Not only is it beyond imagining, it simply does not happen in a youth-obsessed world. And yet we know the reality: that sexual needs are normal and require expression in both men and women throughout the entire life span.

Medical discoveries have enabled man to enjoy longevity, not as a neuter in the later years, but as a participant in all the joys of human existence. Nevertheless, there are many fallacies, myths, and stereotypes about sexuality and aging that must be corrected if older persons wish to enjoy the full privileges of age and experience. Myths and fallacies about sexual response pervade every part of the life cycle, but most especially that of the aging. There is a multitude of books on sexuality, but few on the sexual aspects of people in their later years. This resistance to candid examination of the subject is considerable. Not only is sex surrounded by inhibitions and primitive taboos; youth is disdainful of the older generation's interest in sex. Typical is the reaction of offspring of elderly people when they think any sexual activity might be going on or developing with their parents. Those in the older generation themselves often feel guilty if they do feel sexual desire.

One has to keep reminding oneself that, in the period in which these people were growing up, any kind of sexual activity was treated with secrecy and shame. There was none of today's atmosphere of ease and openness. Women were not supposed to respond or even have any sexual desires. A woman presented herself as a bride to her husband, preferably as a virgin, and her total sexuality was for the purpose of procreation. Now that we know women have sexual drives and desires and always have had, it is an interesting retrospect. We know now that many women in the past most assuredly enjoyed sex while keeping it a deep, dark secret. The "respectable" woman was not supposed even to think about sex. Some myths die hard, perhaps because they are adhered to by those who look forward to a respectable reason to terminate their sexual life. They welcome the excuse of age, so to speak.

Therefore, we can conclude that a great deal of emotional resistance faces the findings about sexuality in the later years. I also have found that the fallacies, the prohibitions, and the inhibitions are not just demonstrated by the nonprofessional part of the community; they also are found in the professional community. This frightens me, and I hope it frightens you. Apparently some of these professionals are not aware of the research that has been done. Perhaps they do not realize that they should have this information at their fingertips when dealing with people in the later age group. The dangerous stereotype of the sexless older years is not only part of the lay community; it is also part of the professional community.

I am not going to say that the research on sexuality in the later years is totally inadequate, but I would say that most of us draw from a pool of research that is rather limited. We can speak of the Duke studies and of Masters and Johnson, but the sample is rather small. Some other studies have been done, but they are few and far between. The professional does not have a pool of information he can turn to which is truly representative of large samples. What does that say? I suppose the first thing is that it must be rather difficult to deal with older research subjects because of a reluctance on their part to be involved. I don't think that is true; I have found them very open and eager to join in any kind of research involving their age group. Or does it tell us that the professional community itself is not really interested in this aspect of research? I really don't know.

Let's consider the Duke University study: the original subjects of the study were 260 community volunteers, men and women, black and white, married and single, all of whom were over 60 at the inception of the study. The inquiry into sexual behavior constituted a part of an overall study conducted by psychiatrists by means of lengthy interviews. This study, like others, indicated a gradual decline of the reported frequency in sexual intercourse with advancing age. The findings were that from 45% to 65% of the subjects between the ages of 60 and 71 still reported engaging in sexual intercourse with some frequency, while only 10% to 20% of the group 78 and over still reported sexual activity.

A rather surprising finding that emerged from the study was that a significant portion, about 15%, showed increased patterns of sexual activity as they grew older. Of the 63 men and 70 women who had stopped having sexual intercourse, the median age for stopping was 68 for men and 60 for the women. However, in assigning responsibility for the cessation of activity, both husbands and wives agreed that the husband was the determining factor.

Let's first consider the findings on the female. Masters and Johnson, in their studies of sex and the aging, conducted the first studies on older females. They studied 61 older women, ranging in age up to 78 years. The results indicated that both the intensity of the physiological response and the rapidity of response to sexual stimulation was reduced with women as the years advanced. The sex flush was more limited and restricted in the older women. There was less lubrication. There was delay in the reaction of the clitoris to direct stimulation. There was a reduction in the orgasmic time, et cetera. But the heartening conclusion of the Masters and Johnson study was that significant sexual capacity and effective sexual performance in these older women was found. The aging female is fully capable of sexual performance and orgasmic response, particularly if she is exposed to regular sexual stimulation. There seem to be no physiological reasons that the frequency of sexual expression found satisfactory for the younger woman should not be carried over into the post-menopausal years. In short, they concluded there is no time limit drawn by the advancing years to female sexuality.

What are some of the factors that affect the female? Once again we place so much emphasis on youth that the climacteric period in many women has many traumatic ramifications. Although a specific age is often cited in relation to menopause, the age for individuals is highly variable. This is because there is not a sudden onset. It is a part of an overall pattern associated with that period. Because of the psychic vulnerability of the American woman (and we can speak only of our own culture since we have no cross-cultural comparisons) during that menopausal period, there may be many emotional crises, such as a fear of loss of attractiveness and fears based on folklore and superstition. As professionals, we must never, never assume that the persons we are speaking to may have this information available; let them tell us what their feelings are. However, the good news is that only about 40% of women going through menopause have any symptoms at all, and not more than 10% or 15% are disturbed enough to seek medical help.

Despite all the evidence to the contrary, we have large numbers of persons who still believe that after the menopause there will be a considerable decrease in sexual satisfaction for whatever psychological or physical reasons. Of course, this has been refuted by the work of Masters and Johnson and other distinguished researchers. Also we can go back to the Kinsey work, which is now over a quarter of a century old. It is still quoted, and I think rightly so, but people forget it was basically a sociological study. The original research of the Kinsey group still seems to be substantiated by similar studies done today. Both those studies and the current ones show that there is no report of loss of satisfaction for the post-menopausal women. On the contrary, for many women there is a gain because they no longer worry about conception.

I won't go into the medical aspect. It is not my field to talk about hormone replacements or steroid replacement or deprivation, but I would suggest that the mind plays a part that is equal, or even greater, than that of the balanced endocrine system in determining the sex drive of women of the post-menopausal period of their lives. If endocrine factors alone were responsible for sexual behavior in post-menopausal women (whether the menopause is caused by surgical or natural means) there should be a relatively uniform response to the decrease and ultimate withdrawal of sex hormones. However, there are no established reaction patterns to sex steroid variations. For instance, clinical symptoms in menopausal distress vary tremendously between individuals, and for that matter within the same individual as the demand arises for increased mental or physical activity.

Of course, there are several mechanical factors that are occasioned by endocrine imbalance and result indirectly in painful intercourse. Many women who have never been discomforted by sexual activity complain of physical distress during or shortly after coital connection in the immediate post-menopausal years. Intercourse can become severely painful during the penetration phase or extended coital connection. Intercourse may be followed by a vaginal burning, and irritation on urination, and for some women these symptoms may continue for 24 to 36 hours after sexual connection. These symptoms of burning and irritation usually result from a marked thinning of the vaginal mucosa and a reduction of involuntary distensibility of the vaginal barrel. The natural ability to lubricate the vaginal barrel effectively may be reduced or the reaction time slowed by women beyond their middle fifties.

Even more important to maintaining sexual capacity is the regularity of sexual expression, for the aging woman much more than for her younger counterpart; such opportunities have a significant effect on her sexual performance. As you may recall, Masters and Johnson found that three women past sixty were repeatedly observed to expand and lubricate the vagina effectively despite the obvious senile thinning of the vaginal walls and shrinking of the major labia. But these women had maintained regular coital connection at least once or twice per week for their entire adult lives.

We know the aging woman's vagina undergoes specific changes and these should be described in some detail before attempting to establish the difference in vaginal response to sexual tensions between younger and older women. After the woman has undergone the normal menopausal evolution of ovarian sex steroid reduction, changes develop in the target areas—the labia, vagina, the uterus and the breasts. The well stimulated healthy vagina of a 30 year old woman has an entirely different appearance than that of a steroid-starved woman in the 61-70 group. After the ovaries cease or grossly reduce steroid production, the walls of the vaginal barrel begin to involute; they lose the well-corrugated, thickened, reddish-purple appearance. The walls of the senile vaginal barrel become tissue-paper thin and change to a light pinkish color. Upon examination it would appear that the introduction of any object would actually pierce the wall as if it were a tissue.

Frequently women from five to ten years postmenses who experience infrequent coition—and infrequently means once a month or less—and who do not masturbate with regularity, have difficulty in accommodating a penis during intercourse. It is also true that younger women deprived of coital opportunity for long periods of time may have to contend with a slower rate of vaginal lubrication and restricted vaginal barrel expansion during a first return to coital connection. However, their difficulties are far less pronounced than those of older women in similar circumstances of coital deprivation, and their full physiological response by coital stimulation is established far more rapidly. There is another manifestation of steroid imbalance and the sexual response patterns of the aging female. As women age and lose their sex steroid levels, uterine contractions occurring in orgasms frequently become painful; this is important to be aware of in counseling because these women may be hesitant to bring it up. The actual degree of distress varies from time to time and from woman to woman, but when experienced, this painful uterine cramping develops during, as well as subsequent to, orgasmic expression. While these uterine contractions occur in women of all ages experiencing orgasmic response, younger women rarely have the accompanying physical discomfort that reaches the level of clinical distress. In passing, I might mention again the original studies of Masters and Johnson relative to what takes place during intercourse. The reason that we know so specifically about the uterine contractions is that, of the original sample of women who were in research, three volunteered to return for evaluation by Masters and Johnson during the delivery of their babies; and their first stages of labor were evaluated with the same equipment that was used for evaluation of their sexual response when they were in the original sample. It was found that data relative to the contractions of the uterus during the first stages of labor could be superimposed over the data describing the contractions of the subjects during the original research on orgasmic response.

But beyond sixty, some women are so distressed with these contractions that they purposely avoid orgasmic response and coital connection if possible. The simple fact remains, however, that if opportunity for regularity of coital exposure is created and maintained, the elderly woman suffering from all the vaginal stigmas of sex steroid starvation still will retain a far higher capacity of sex performance than her female counterpart who doesn't have similar coital opportunities. We have seen that endocrine starvation has an indirect influence, but certainly not absolute control, over the female sexual capacity or performance. Steroid starvation also has an indirect influence upon female sexual drive.

Kinsey's group noted that a large part of the sex drive in the postmenopausal age is directly related to the sexual habits established during the procreative years. The interview material of Masters and Johnson also suggests that a woman who had had a happy, well-adjusted, and stimulating marriage may progress through the menopausal and postmenopausal years with little or no interruption in the frequency of or interest in sexual activity. Additionally, social and economic security are major factors in many women's successful adjustment in their later years. Needless to say, an increasingly large segment of the female population is diametrically opposite to the reasonably adjusted individual we have just described. If a woman has been plagued with a nonorgasmic response or by a lack of regular, recurrent sexually satisfying coital activity during her active reproductive years, there is reason to believe that the advent of the post-menopausal years may serve to decrease the sex drive and to make the idea of any sexual expression increasingly repugnant. This individual, of course, uses the excuse of advancing years to avoid the personal embarrassment of inadequate sexual performance or the frustrations of unresolved sexual tensions. What I am saying is that there are many men and women who, through no fault of their own, do look forward to a respectable reason for the ending of sexual relations. That applies particularly to those who have always felt that sex was something they "had to go through." Many unconsciously welcome the advancing years to abandon the function that has been unpleasant since childhood.

What of sexual activity of women in the 70+ age group? Unfortunately, this is influenced by the factor of male availability. When available, the female's marital partners average four years older, but many of the older husbands in this age group are, of course, suffering from the multiple physical disabilities that come within that age group. This sometimes makes sexual activity for these men either unattractive or in some cases physically impossible. Thus, the wives who might well be interested in some regularity of heterosexual expression are denied the opportunity due to the husband's infirmities.

And what about the male? Let's look first at the Masters and Johnson work. The data we had at the Foundation were based on men from their early 50's to 89 years of age. It came from 39 men – which admittedly is a small sample. The availability of research subjects is limited, so we still need to do some larger studies. As was true for their aging female counterparts, it was extremely difficult at that time to elicit much cooperation from even the small group of men. Masters' and Johnson's work goes back well over 11 to 15 years, and the material must be accepted in the light of an admittedly inadequate subject population. This is particularly true of the results of men over 70. However, the returns from the limited number of aging males provide the opportunity for comparison with the patterns of sexual response firmly established for younger men, and will permit, of course, some of the superficial considerations of the effects of aging process and sexual physiology. Also included, by the way, were men of 51 to 60. They were included in the discussion in the study to provide a parallel to the menopausal women's response patterns.

In the males studied by Masters and Johnson evidence was found that the frequency of sexual response lessened with age. Erection took much longer. There was a longer period needed to reach ejaculation, and ejaculation lacked the same force and duration. The sex flush was largely reduced and greater time was required before another erection could be reached. There were also fewer morning erections. But once again, Masters and Johnson added, there is every reason to believe that regularity of sexual expression, coupled with adequate physical well-being and healthy mental orientation to the aging process, will combine to provide a sexually stimulated climate within the marriage. This climate will in turn include reduced sexual tension and will provide adequate capacity for sexual performance that frequently may extend to and beyond the 80 year level.

Sometimes in my counseling, however, a male will come in and will complain that it takes him five or six minutes to get an erection. When I ask him his age, he might say he will soon be 58. I can say "Congratulations," because for many males of this age it takes 30 to 40 minutes; that's a fact. We know that as we age our physical ability to perform in athletic events diminishes. A male will accept the fact that even if he was a good athlete as a youngster, he can't be as good at age 60. But males will not allow that difference in the sexual area. They remember that as a youngster they responded fast, and they still want it to go the same way. There are many ways you can approach this in counseling. The one I believe has validity is simply to suggest that the individual become more sophisticated, more selective.

There is the constant question of the advisability of the administration of sex hormones for the male. Will they have a beneficial effect? Masters and Johnson note that the obvious elevation of eroticism which may occur after hormonal replacement for males is not a direct result of the hormone's effect, but rather a secondary result of the obvious improvement of the total body economy and of a renewed sense of well-being. That is hard to sort out, but I think that kind of evaluation is valuable in terms of the controversy over the advisability of administering hormones to males. None of us can rule out the placebo effect.

The most important fact for the maintenance of effective sexuality for the aging male is consistency of actual sexual expression. When the male is stimulated to high sexual output during the formative years and a similar tenor of activity is established in the 31 to 40 range, his middle age and later years usually are marked by constantly-recurring physiological evidence of maintained sexuality. The geriatric sample of men currently interested in relatively high levels of sexual expression reports activity levels similar to those of their formative years. Also, it is interesting that it does not seem to matter which level of sexual expression has been employed, as long as high levels of activity were maintained. This means that it didn't make any difference whether it was intercourse or masturbation as long as the activity was maintained.

The influence of sexual inadequacy in the human male does take an upturn after age 50. As might be expected, secondary impotence increases markedly after this age and continues to increase with each additional decade. During the last few years' experience in therapy for sexual inadequacy, 83% of impotent males have been past 40 at the onset of impotence and three out of every four were over 50 at its onset. Of real interest — and this is an important plus factor — is the fact that the male over 50 can be trained out of the secondary impotence in a high percentage of cases. We find that as the sedentary male over 50 can be reconstituted, likewise a potent aging male's responsive ability, dormant for physical or social reasons, can be restimulated if the male wishes to return to active sexual practice and has a partner interested in sexual performance. If a 70 or even 80 year-old male is in adequate health, little is needed to support adequacy of sexual performance other than some physiological outlet and a psychological reason to react to some sexual interest. If the elevated level of sexual activity is maintained from earlier years and neither acute nor chronic physical incapacity intervenes, males are usually able to continue some form of active sexual expression into their seventies and even eighties. Even if the coital activity has been avoided for long periods of time, men in these age groups can be returned to effective sexual functions if adequate stimulation is instituted. Of course, the essential factor is that they have an interesting partner available.

Once again, the aging male's sexual capacity and performance varies among individuals and across time in a particular individual. As we said before, other studies along with the Masters and Johnson studies show that the socially essential environment within which the male lives during sexually formative years is the key to continuing functioning in the later years. Kinsey suggested this prospect back in 1948, and of course the present studies continue to substantiate this. If this well-adjusted pattern of frequency is maintained earlier, it will continue.

"How often should I be doing it? What's normal?" There isn't such a thing as normal; it's what is right for you. Research-wise there are a few important factors. With rare exceptions a male over 60 usually will be satisfied completely with one or at the most two ejaculations a week, regardless of the number of coital opportunities or the sexual demands of his female partner. Many men in their middle or late fifties or in their sixties say they cannot redevelop penile erection unless there is an interim period of twelve to twenty-four hours after ejaculation. Those who achieve a relatively early return to erection may have lost their ejaculatory urge and are physically content to serve their female partner to the completion of the woman's sexual demands without recurrent ejaculatory interest.

One of the things that is very important to bring out when discussing the sexual activity in the older male and female is that it is very difficult to sort out the psychological facts from the physiological ones. This has to be the new direction of research. We can turn to animal studies of sexual drive and age to attempt to increase our understanding. For example, if the old male white rat has had his old lady white rat friend for quite a while, and you take her out and bring a new young white rat in, he'll be mounting all over the place. He seems to get back to where he was earlier. But the old male rat eventually goes back to the same level of sexual activity that he had with his previous lady rat. The point is that upon the introduction of a new partner there is renewed activity.

I get upset when I see in a popular magazine an article that advises, "Go out and get a new sexual partner; put new interest in your sex life." I suppose it does happen many times, because the fact is that after people have been together for many decades, and certain levels of boredom have set in, the introduction of a new sexual partner often causes the erection to take place more rapidly. But as the male continues with the new partner, he will eventually return to the same level of functioning that he had with his previous partner. For that reason I don't find the suggestion of extra marital activity a valid one for reconstituting lively sexual activity.

Now what is responsible for the progressive loss of responsiveness in the later years? Monotony, resulting from repetitious sexual activities, usually translated into boredom with a partner may be one cause. Many people in middle age, for example, were instructed that there is only one proper position. Can you imagine what it must be like to try only one position during many years of married life? We must also consider that there is quite often a preoccupation with economic pursuits and career. This contributes to mental and physical fatigue. The middle-aged group are the decision makers of our culture. Responsibility and demands increase while the level of energy is decreasing. These are very real things, but people often are not prepared to meet them in terms of what is happening to them. They try to deny it; they try to over compensate. This will, of course, affect the sexual components of their lives. Sometimes there is overindulgence in drink and food. Masters and Johnson found that secondary impotence developing in the late forties and early fifties often has a very direct association with excessive alcohol consumption. By alcoholic consumption, I don't mean to intimate that there is a direct one-to-one relationship. Usually, the situation is one in which the alcohol is enough to cause the man to experience impotency; then he goes into the fear of failure syndrome. Another problem situation may result from the physical and mental infirmities of either spouse. Of course, this is sometimes multiplied when the individual fails to get the necessary guidance or gets negative and discouraging advice.

Those who went to medical school 20 or more years ago did not have sexuality included in the curriculum. A man who is 50 may seek advice from his doctor. He may tell the doctor about his difficulties with erection only to be consoled with, "John, you are getting old." That's tragic; not only is the response inappropriate but the man in the white coat who knows supposedly everything has reaffirmed the fear of the individual. Such little phrases used by the doctor may leave a very heavy impact on the patient. There is a real crisis when a male experiences impotency. Results can range from a general level of anxiety right down to deep depression.

I don't know what this tells us about our culture. Perhaps it tells us that the male ties up so much of his self-image in his ability to function sexually that when a loss of erection does occur it can be, for some, a very ego-shattering experience. Sometimes the wife does not react adequately, so the husband withdraws completely. The wife doesn't know what to say or to do; it depends on their level of communication. A tremendous range of reactions can occur within both partners upon onset of impotency.

One of the things that we should not ignore is the sex needs of the unmarried. Professionals like yourself can allay the guilt and anxiety of the woman in her later years who tells you that she is masturbating and asks whether she is reverting to infantile behavior. It is wonderful that people like yourself are available to reaffirm the facts for them, not only to "give them permission" but to suggest that it is obvious as a result of research that it has beneficial effects. Whatever level of efficiency and proficiency that a person has, either as a physician or as a member of any helping professions, dealing with the older age group takes real skill as well as background and experience. Many people find it very difficult to talk about sex to anyone, even an authority figure. For the older age group it is particularly important that the counselor or physician be at ease and non-judgmental.

One of the first things that we all can agree is necessary is a good history. I am not talking about a medical history. It is a tragedy that many elderly people go to a doctor who does a very fine medical history, but in a rather detached way. He asks the questions and marks the answers. This is not what the person really needs at that time. The whole attitude of a medical history becomes very impersonal. It does not invite elderly people to talk about a problem, sexual or otherwise, that may be part of their lives. I am not saying anything particularly negative about the attitude of the medical profession; that's the way physicians are trained. They look for some kind of pathology; as a result of this the person may have some very real concerns which are not brought up in the medical visit. Whenever I do a sexual history − after I have gone through my routine and the people have told me all about their condition and their sex life and about all parts of their life that they feel good about having been able to talk about − I always ask at the end, "Is there anything else that might be important for me to know − something you might want to say?" Very often this is when I get some of the most valuable material.

I suggest when you counsel for the sexual aspects of people in their later years that you see both parties. Some people don't take a history of a person in later years because they are operating on all sorts of peculiar assumptions: they wouldn't remember, or "We'd better find some physiological reason here." But people in their later years are delighted to go through their history with you. It shows them your concern as another person. The history might reveal that they have had a number of marriages. They may have come from a background which is a little different or unique in terms of people who are younger. They may have come from a staunch, religious background in which certain things were not permissible. You might even find out what material they have been reading. Sometimes they have been exposed to all kinds of misinformation. Don't assume they don't remember their early sexual history — you bet they do. They can tell you in great detail the early sexual aspects of their life. Regardless in what age group, we have to look for what is happening in the personal relationship with these two people.

The concern of both the physical examination and the sexual history can have positive results. A warm, permissive approach to both the physical examination and the sexual history can build confidence and reduce tension. A lot of people say to me, "How can you approach the sexual history before you have been in therapy with the person for quite some time?" No problem. I find that after a brief interview, and establishing the specific understanding that it is privileged communication and that the information will not be brought to the attention of the mate, I get a very thorough sexual history. Maybe I'm kidding myself — but I don't think so. They seem delighted to talk to someone who is willing to listen and who is qualified to deal with the subject; it is a catharsis for them. Finally, all is out after all these years.

One other thing must be said about many older couples: if they have had a poor relationship all through the early years, then I am afraid that with the advance in years the problems seem to compound. That is sad. I cannot tell you that the prognosis is at all good for an older couple who have had a poor marriage and are facing sexual dysfunction for the first time. It is sad that they have waited so long for counseling, but we never tell them that. Sometimes the problems that were there earlier are magnified and intensified by the difficulties that arise at a later time.

However, your next case may present an opposite situation. If the couple has had a good marriage over the years, they already have established an attitude that they are going to work together as a team to resolve the new problems. For many people in their later years, the sexual problem may have arisen for the first time in their lives; it may be something they have not faced before. But having faced other problems major and/or minor, they usually feel they can face this one with equanimity.

If the subject couple has had a good relationship over the years and sincerely wish to help each other, then the counselor is most helpful in the role of authority for facts and truth. He is the communications medium through which they learn to talk to each other. And given the facts that the counselor should have at his fingertips, they should be able to work out their problems and between them attain a happy level of sexual response.

Treatment, of course, should follow the same pattern as the history-taking interview, i.e., starting with the medical aspects. Only after the physiology is known should counseling begin. If each history has been taken separately, then counseling should be along the principles pioneered by Masters and Johnson. These, though originally for younger people, are just as effective for the elderly, whatever the sexual distress may be.

And despite millions in advertising to the contrary, no amount of "iron" will rejuvenate one's blood, be it young blood or old. "Tired blood," a euphemism for sexual fatigue or any fatigue (if you believe the advertiser), may be the basis for many problems of sexual dysfunction. Fatigue, both mental and physical, is a very real problem in any age group, though the professional will see more of it in older people. The physician treating such problems may diagnose them as anemia, glandular dysfunction, or malnutrition and prescribe accordingly. Proper treatment can and has reconstituted sexual activity in thousands of older people.

Then there is the question every gerontologist must ultimately consider: how well has the couple weathered the storms of middle-age, the woman's menopause, the man's frustrations and waning sexuality, boredom, and all the countless ills that "man is heir to"? If they have reached that "golden age" the poets sing about, who's to say that sex is neither necessary nor possible? Or if there is a little spark left, who's to say it is not "normal"? Who, indeed? But the fact is there are still people, mostly young, who think sex for a senior is not "nice." Oldsters frequently ask their physicians for help with a problem of gradually lessened potency. And the doctors, instead of making tests to see if anything can be done medically, too often dismiss the idea as inconsequential.

Why do people, including some professionals, deny the existence and importance of sexuality in old age? We are becoming more and more tolerant of sexual self-determination for virtually every segment of the population — the young, the married, the singles, the variants — yet we let the puritanical moralities and out-dated ideas of past generations continue to influence our attitudes toward sex for older men and women.

The French (naturally!) have a word for it, *"Si jeunesse savait,* etc.,*"* often repeated in English: "If youth only knew; if age only could!" and what with all the emphasis today on sex education for the young, perhaps this idea should be added to the curriculum: there is no scientific reason why sex should not be an important factor every day of one's life from birth to death.

References

Masters, W. M., & Johnson, V. E. *Human sexual response.* Boston: Little, Brown, 1966.

Master, W. M. & Johnson, V. E. *Human sexual inadequacy.* Boston: Little, Brown, 1970.

Rubin, I. *Sexual life after sixty.* New York: Basic Books, 1965.

A Program
of Sexual Liberation
and Growth
in the Elderly

8

Mary Ann P. Sviland

Very recently a positive shift of increased sophistication and public concern has arisen in the area of gerosexuality. Sexuality in the aging may finally be emerging as a meritorious area for sex education and therapy focus. But the persistent common myth that sexuality is the domain of the young still resigns many senior citizens to premature impotency, frustration, self-depreciation, loneliness, and depression. Helping older persons improve their sexual function and achieve their biological destiny is not an end in itself, but is a means of fulfilling a deeper core — the timeless need of all humans for intimacy and love. Thwarted sexuality and the lack of an intimate and empathetic relationship, with concomitant feelings of loneliness and unwantedness, may contribute more to depression in the elderly, currently diagnosed as involutional, than previously assumed.

This article describes a sexual therapy program specifically tailored towards helping elderly persons become sexually liberated. This program has successfully allowed persons over the age of sixty to overcome sexual lethargy, decrease their sexual inhibitions, and expand their repertoire of sexual behaviors to conform to recently liberalized sexual mores (Sviland, 1975a).

Through successful attitude restructuring, some couples on this program who maintain a playful, unhurried atmosphere during sex have developed an increase in sexuality that may even exceed their earlier age activity (Sviland, 1976). This is not surprising since we know a wide gap exists for most persons, regardless of age, between sexual potential and average sexual performance. Furthermore, the potential for sexual growth with aging was reported earlier in a longitudinal study at Duke University which found that approximately fifteen percent of the subjects over sixty years of age grew sexually over the ten-year time span of the study (Verwoerdt, Pfeiffer & Wang, 1969).

Before describing the objectives and methods of this treatment program, it is important to understand some major psychosocial issues of sexuality which influence sexual behavior in the elderly. These include cultural stereotyping and myths on aging sexuality, current knowledge of sexual behavior in the elderly, and restrictive cultural and physiological factors limiting elderly sexuality.

Cultural Stereotyping and Myths on Aging Sexuality

Sexual discrimination against the elderly still exists in this era of expanding sexual understanding and liberation of attitudes and behaviors. Society finds amusing or insignificant the sexual needs of elderly persons. Jokes involving old people and sex bring inevitable laughter and are a comedian's stock in trade. Typical of a media "joke" which reinforces negative stereotyping of aging sexuality is this comment made by a famous gray haired comic on television, "I started out the other night to paint the town red, but then I found that I had run out of paint." About two-thirds of the jokes dealing with older persons are negative, with major themes of sexual decline, physical decline, and loss of attractiveness (Richman, 1977; Davies, 1977).

The word "agism" was recently coined to signify the profound prejudice and biased stereotyping towards the elderly which is as bad as or worse than racism or sexism (Butler, 1975a). Fallacies and stereotypes that abound in the public mind include the following: most elderly become infirm and live in rest homes; older people think and move slowly, become emotionally disengaged and are bored with life; senility is inevitable; the aged are inflexible, unproductive and in essence lonely, poor, bedridden or incompetent. Yet in fact only 5% of the elderly are institutionalized. In a study involving retired college professors it was found that most of their memory and cognitive functions were intact and equivalent to an average younger age group (Schaie & Strother, 1968). In essence, age magnifies but does not radically alter personality. A sociable, energetic, flexible young person with many interests will become an involved, sociable, energetic, flexible old person.

Similarly, common myths and stereotypes about elderly sexuality include: aging inevitably leads to impotence; many women lose sexual interest following menopause; sexual frequency lessens with age. However, only 10% of the impotence seen in aging males is of a nonreversible permanent form (Butler, 1975b). Much impotency diagnosed as organic attributable to aging is actually attributable to such psychological and environmental variables as performance anxiety, loss of interest, or parter unavailability. Many women demonstrate an increase in sex drive following menopause (Masters & Johnson, 1966). As stated earlier, some persons over 60 years show increasing patterns of sexual activity (Verwoerdt, Pfeiffer, & Wang, 1969; Sviland, 1976). To date, little effort has been directed toward helping older persons have the same sexual freedom and expression which is afforded the young. Rather, within many segments of this society, the elderly are forced into mandatory retirement from sexual activity. Imposed social barriers to sexual expression range from psychologically subtle family coldness towards the elderly person's social companions to physically direct segregation of husbands and wives in retirement facilities and nursing care homes.

Primary opposition to sexuality in the aged has been attributed to adult children who view their aged parents' normal urges for intimacy and romance as a threat of social disgrace and/or onset of second childhood (Dean, 1966). Denial of parental sexuality is much greater for the mother than for the father and generalizes to unacceptance of sexuality towards all elderly females (Claman, 1966). Mateless parents who express loneliness are told to take up a hobby or are pressed into household services instead of being encouraged to reenter the mainstream of life via another intimate relationship. Often repression of parental sexuality stems from disillusionment and hidden resentment. Some adult children who inhibited their own sexuality for many years in deference to their parents' restrictive sexual values simply cannot tolerate the feelings of betrayal and loss engendered by their parents' turned-about, sexually liberated values and behaviors (Sviland, in press). The dread of parental sexual acting out is readily observed in the strict nursing home prohibitions of physical contact, designed to please the bill-paying adult children, despite the fact that free acceptance of sexuality in homes for the aged has been advocated as humanistic (Kassell, 1974).

However, as adult children in our society are becoming less personally involved with nearby parents as well as living farther away than previously, the mobile elderly are able to become more sexually open, free, and independent of family goodwill regarding their sexual behavior. To date, no case has been seen in this program where an older person's sexuality was being inhibited through opposition of adult children. Rather, one frequently sees many pathetic instances where a married person felt guilty about still wanting to make love to a disinterested spouse who indignantly insists they were too old and should act their age. The most vociferous opponents of elderly sexuality can be elderly persons themselves who have a compelling need to defend their own antisexual stance. For persons with lifelong sexual conflict or disinterest, age provides a plausible alibi to release themselves from anxiety-provoking sexual situations. Many single older persons are also encountered who are ashamed of their continuing urge to masturbate because of partner unavailability. Since the feelings and behaviors of older persons are related to societal expectations, many elderly people feel guilty about healthy sexual feelings because they are unacceptable to themselves, the physician or other people around them (Newman & Nichols, 1966). Psychotherapists, counselors, and sex educators may also need to examine their own social biases regarding aging sexuality and increase their understanding of elderly sexual capability to foster a supporting climate for the resolution of healthy sexual function in their elderly clients.

Current Knowledge of Sexual Behavior in the Elderly

The discrimination towards elderly sexuality is reflected in sexual research. Only three out of 1700 pages in the two Kinsey reports are devoted to older people (Claman, 1966). The Masters and Johnson (1966) study of sexual response included only 31 male and female subjects beyond age sixty, in a total population of 694 subjects. People over 60 comprise 26.7% of the total population over 18 years yet had only a 4.5% representation in this sexual response cycle study. Part of this poor representation was caused by difficulty in obtaining cooperative elderly subjects. Apparently societal strictures leave the elderly defensive about disclosing their sexual life. Yet older persons remain terribly confused and vitally interested in information about norms of sexuality in the elderly population (Feigenbaum, Lowenthal, & Tries, 1967).

Some of the statistics on elderly sexuality may be misleading. The observed decline of sexuality with age may be reflecting psychological or social variables that occur concomitantly with aging rather than age *per se.* A glaring omission in the studies of Kinsey and later colleagues is the lack of exploration of the emotional aspects of the sexual relationship (Berezin, 1969). Sex behavior does not necessarily correlate with physical drive state. Variables such as affection, tenderness, and warmth could enhance sexuality while an ego deflating argument or physically repellent mate would probably reduce sexuality. Furthermore, previous studies have over-focused on sexual intercourse as a measure of sexual frequency, yet many married people also engage in other forms of sex play to orgasm which they may not choose to disclose openly.

There is good reason to believe that earlier findings do not reflect the sexual patterns of today's elderly. The recent liberalization of sexual values now sanctions sexual behaviors previously viewed as pathological, such as masturbation and oral sex. With new social acceptance, greater frequencies of these behaviors could also be expected to be found in the elderly, as well as the young.

The important point is that prior normative data which may now be outmoded should not be used as a basis for restricting sexuality in the elderly. The phenomenon of regression to the mean extends to sexuality. If a 70 year old man is told that the average orgasm frequency for his age is .9 per week, he would probably not attempt more even if 3 per week is his average functioning capacity. The supernormal frequencies found in some elderly males may more accurately reflect innate capacity and could become the average expectation in a more guiltless, biologically natural culture (Stokes, 1951).

Having noted the research limitations in aging sexuality, the current findings on elderly sexuality will next be described.

Contrary to popular cultural mythology, the greater the sexual interest, activity, and capacity in earlier life, the greater the interest, activity, and capacity in later years (Claman, 1966). Early termination of sexual activities occurs where sex was not important in earlier life (Pfeiffer & Davis, 1972). The physical capacity for sex is highly variable among people. Due to hormonal or other physical influences, some people have a normally low sexual drive state. However, a low sexual drive state due to psychological reasons can be reactivated (Sviland, 1975b).

Frequency of morning erections, a sign of physical and sexual vigor, does not significantly decline until the male is 66 years or older (Kinsey, Pomeroy, & Martin, 1948). Yet many American males show onset of sexual difficulties around 50 years of age or earlier. The ability to have a morning erection clearly establishes a psychological rather than physical basis for impotence. One major psychological basis of secondary impotence in the male is worry over sexual failure (Kaplan, 1974). Some males in their 50's and 60's abstain from sex to avoid painful feelings of frustration, anxiety, or depression over their declining sexual performance (Kaplan, 1974). Sexual problems experienced by aging males are generally reversible. Inability to achieve erection, loss of erection, and retarded ejaculation difficulties have been successfully eliminated in the elderly male when their common basis, performance anxiety, was systematically removed (Sviland, 1975b; 1976).

Contrary to male sexuality which typically shows a steady decline from peak responsiveness around age 18, female sexuality in our culture reaches peak responsiveness in the late 30's and early 40's and can maintain this level into the sixties. Elderly women remain capable of enjoying multiple orgasms (Kaplan, 1974). Following menopause, many women show an increase in sexual interest which concurs with the theoretical increase in libido that should occur because androgen action is now unopposed by estrogen (Kaplan, 1974). Women in their 50's and 60's who discontinue sex abstain primarily for sociological and psychological reasons, not biological factors, since they do not seek partner replacements unless they are unusually attractive and secure (Kaplan, 1974).

Good health and receptive partner are crucial variables to active sexuality. Seven out of 10 healthy married elderly couples were found to be sexually active, some into their late 80's (Swartz, 1966). In contrast only 7% of the single, divorced, or widowed persons over 60 years were found to be sexually active (Newman & Nichols, 1966). By the age of 70, 70% of married males had a mean sexual frequency of .9 per week, with some males maintaining frequency of three times per week (Kinsey, Pomeroy, & Martin, 1948; Newman & Nichols, 1960). By age 75, 50% of married males still engaged in intercourse (Claman, 1966). Similarly, at 60 years, 70% of married females but only 12% of postmarried females engage in intercourse. Masturbation incidence was higher for widowed and divorced females, with 25% of single females aged 70 still masturbating (Christenson & Gagnon, 1965), which attests to the strength of sexuality in women irrespective of male initiation.

Restrictive Cultural and Physiological Factors Limiting Elderly Sexuality

We are realizing that sexual decline in the elderly is less a factor of biology than an artifact of social prohibitions and lack of willing-partner availability. Although there are some cultural restrictions on the elderly male, his sexuality is primarily limited by physical factors. In contrast, those elderly females who remain physically capable and responsive are primarily limited from sexual expression by cultural factors. Understanding this distinction is necessary for a more rational approach to sexuality in the aged.

The majority of the elderly males in this culture experience reduced sexual stamina which adversely affects sexual behavior. Sexual changes may include: decreased orgasm frequency, longer refractory periods following orgasm, loss of awareness of pending orgasm, and greater need for direct stimulation for arousal (Kaplan, 1974). A shift in the sexual pattern with the female taking a more active role may be required to increase compatibility and to maximize the aging male's sexual capabilities.

Since aging does not substantially affect sexual capacity of elderly females, compared to elderly males, it is cultural factors, such as the double standard, which impede sexual actualization in elderly females. The majority of elderly women are faced with approximately a decade of matelessness since they tend to marry males four years older and the life expectancy for males is seven years shorter. Females outnumber males 138.5 to 100 at age 65 and 156.2 to 100 at age 75 (Pfeiffer & Davis, 1972). Thus, elderly females glut the social market place, which makes it easier for widowed males to date or remarry.

Various solutions have been proposed to eliminate the elderly widow's sexual dilemma, from polygamy to initially marrying a man younger than she (Kassel, 1966; Dean 1972). But another logical solution would be to alleviate the current double standard that denies elderly females the same access to younger partners that elderly males have. While older men are considered "distinguished" and are admired for attracting a younger female, older women are considered "homely" and are criticized for distracting a younger male.

But there is no further need to view sexual contact with an older woman as physically repugnant, a condition which stems from our cult of equating youth and beauty. Furthermore, some of the physical signs of aging in either sex, the flabbiness and the wrinkles, are due to poor body caretaking, not the aging process. Many elderly people who lived prudently are remarkably attractive without the physical signs we attribute to old age. Both women and men should be allowed to pick their life partners on the sole basis of compatibility. This would make acceptable the relationship of the younger male with an older female as depicted to the limits in the film *Harold and Maude.* Age discrepant relationships do not necessarily indicate psychopathology for either party. In dealing with the expanding geriatric population and their sexual needs, society will have to take a more liberalized view regarding alternate life styles. People should be allowed to choose their mates on the basis of psychological compatibility, not preconceived standards of propriety or normalcy (Sviland, 1975a). Otherwise, the young will have to live with the constraints they place upon their elders.

Sexual Therapy to Help the Elderly Become Sexually Liberated

Many therapists and sexual therapy programs are now directing themselves to enhancing sexuality (Kaplan, 1974). Therapy modalities, which range from weekend sexual workshops directed to body awareness and non-demand mutual pleasuring to the more traditional techniques, are helping elderly people obtain a more fulfilling sexual adjustment. Their needs are no less important sexually and no less desirable socially than the needs of the younger people.

This article describes a sex therapy program in a medical hospital setting and in private practice. It was primarily designed for couples over the age of sixty with a basically sound marriage relationship who want to shed their sexual inhibitions and expand their repertoire of sexual behaviors in line with recently liberated mores.

Raised in a more prohibitive era, they want to erase still prevalent internal taboos about such activities as oral-genital sex, masturbation, or sex for pleasure. The program focuses on attitude restructuring, both in the removal of sexually negative self-labels and in relationship enhancement. For it is the climate of granting self-permission to be sexual, coupled with feelings of mutual acceptance, warmth, and physical desire, that allows natural, spontaneous sexuality to flourish and grow.

Couples are seen weekly for one hour and given homework assignments which may range from romantic "dates" to specific sexual exercises. Individually kept daily logs supply the therapist with information on task success, self perceptions, and relationship conflicts. The treatment eclectically combines educational materials, behavior modification and traditional psychotherapy principles according to the needs and goals of each couple.

Sexual values and capabilities differ markedly among the elderly. Therefore the therapist never advocates specific behaviors but helps each couple explore their fantasies and set their own goals. The couples are given permission to experiment with as wide a range of sexual behaviors as desired. Later they discard or incorporate these behaviors into their sexual patterns according to their own values of meaningfulness.

The program can be generally divided into the following steps:

Initial Assessment

The couple is seen together, then individually for one session to explore: a) current sex life; b) subjective feelings about current sex life; c) marital dynamics; d) degree of attitude change mutually desired; and e) definition of goals and probable therapy time required.

Mutuality in sexual goals is a major problem in sex therapy with the elderly. Typically in goal incompatibility problem cases, one partner wants to become more sexually expansive while the other wants to avoid any form of sex. Many dysfunctional males avoid sex because of fear of more failure and further painful feelings of inadequacy and shame. The wife's disinterest in sex may be based on years of lack of enjoyment and orgastic dysfunction due to the husband's insensitivity to her needs, or from a chronic deteriorated relationship. As one wife stated, "After twenty thousand boring repetitions, I've earned the right to retire." Therapy directed to opening communication and enhancing a warm relationship must precede sexual expansion techniques. Sexual therapy is contraindicated over traditional psychotherapy where deeper intrapsychic conflicts result in sexual avoidance.

Granting Permission to be Sexual

The primary therapy goal is to increase sexual satisfaction through the acceptance of one's sexuality without guilt or shame. The therapist becomes a stronger authority figure than the super-ego in granting permission for sexual curiosity and in warmly reinforcing each exploratory movement. The basic therapeutic attitude engendered is that sex can be playful and enjoyable, another way of expressing affection. Sex does not have to be either a ritual or a sacrament. One does what one wants when one feels like it.

Working Through Obstructive Marital Dynamics

Sexual behavior is examined from the wider perspective of the total marital relationship. Negative transactions and hidden resentments must be removed before sexual therapy can begin. Many times the bedroom is a battleground for hostilities and resentments arising elsewhere in the relationship. Improved sexual adjustment is improbable while the partners are occupied in power struggles, uncooperativeness, and withholding sexually satisfying behaviors. Increased sexual gratification requires a shift toward positive feelings about the partner, and will not automatically occur from technique improvement alone. One case comes to mind where the couple was locked into a typical repetitive, destructive, endless transaction. The wife, playing the sexual script game of "Rapo" (Berne, 1964), would be extremely seductive until the husband took the bait and made a sexual overture, wherein she could reject him indignantly, stating that he only wanted sex from her. This script was compatible to the husband's script of "Kick Me". Although the wife repeatedly requested sexuality in the context of romance and affection, the husband remained consistently blunt, matter of fact and insensitive, sabotaging the romantic homework assignments. The sexual script outcomes of outrage in the wife and anger at rejection in the husband served as fuel for revenge in a more pervasive marital power struggle. Although these partners were able easily to liberate attitudinally and expand their repertoire of sexual behavior, sexual adjustment could not take place until this transactional dynamic was broken through and there was a loosening of the competitiveness and power struggle in the sexual scene.

Enhancing Direct Communication

Many older persons, raised in an era that stressed face-saving and role-playing, have difficulty in directly expressing their feelings, needs, and wishes. Many older persons are embarrassed to directly express sexual desires but rather remain silent, hoping their partners are gifted with ESP. Many older women were culturally trained to be passive and non-assertive generally as well as sexually, but the price of "people-pleasing" is resentment and covert hostility.

Assertion training techniques such as: requesting behavior, giving and accepting compliments, dealing with criticism, saying no, and disarming anger may be demonstrated to help the partners become more comfortably authentic (Alberti & Emmons, 1970; Fensterheim & Baer, 1975). As the partners develop greater understanding and acceptance of each other's needs and feelings, a new intimacy and warmth emerges.

Sexual Attitude Restructuring

The most difficult task in sexual therapy is convincing people that they are more sexual than they act. As with most potential behaviors a wide discrepancy exists between real sexual capacity and actual sexual performance. This problem is compounded in sexual therapy with older persons because of the plethora of misinformation describing the "inevitable" sexual dysfunctions that "should" occur with age. The old maxim "we are what we think we are" is especially pertinent to sexuality because values and attitudes, not physical arousal states, regulate sexual behavior.

The elderly female is taught to become more excitable and orgasmic to different types of sexual advances from her mate. The elderly male is taught to readily generate erections, reobtain lost erections, and enhance orgasm frequency. During the course of therapy some couples develop an increase in sexuality that exceeds their earlier activity.

Increasing Physical Attractiveness

In cases where the relationship is dull because the couple take each other for granted and do not satisfy each other's romantic needs, techniques are added to increase physical attractiveness and to bring the quality of a love affair into the marriage. Both describe the kinds of clothing, grooming, and behavior that would make the partner more attractive.

The husband may be told, "If your wife was a young secretary, how would you have to look and what would you have to say to get her to take you seriously as a potential lover?" The wife may be told, "If you were widowed and wanted to trap this man in a field of rough competition, how would you have to dress and act and talk to turn him into an ardent suitor?" Simultaneous homework exercises to replicate the playfulness, intrigue and joy of dating may include candlelight dinners, unexpected love notes, flirtatious telephone conversations, picnics and love-making in remote sunny meadows or by their own fireplace, and so forth.

Sex Education Tools

Sex education is an integral component of the therapy program. It is a mistake automatically to assume that older persons understand sexual anatomy, the sexual response cycle, or effective sexual techniques. It is not uncommon to encounter elderly professional men who have never viewed their wife's genitalia or who cannot find the clitoris. In dealing with the varying levels of sexual problems within each couple, the P-LI-SS-IT model (Annon, 1974) including permission giving, limited information and specific suggestions may be effectively employed.

Major facts on elderly sexuality which are frequently unknown include:

The clitoris is an important component of orgasm.

Some post-menopausal women are multi-orgasmic.

Many females require some form of clitoral contact and stimulation for arousal or orgasm and to this end, touching or oral-genital contact are socially acceptable.

The improved ejaculatory control found in aging males allows for longer intercourse before orgasm, which can enhance the female's pleasure.

There is no physical evidence that aging males cannot continue sexual expression with small or even negligible reduction in frequency.

The aging male requires increased direct genital contact for arousal or orgasm and to this end, touching or oral-genital contact are socially acceptable techniques.

Intercourse positions can be varied for maximum enjoyment and all position variations are socially acceptable.

Afterplay enhances satisfaction in the emotional component of sexuality, especially for the female.

Masturbation is a socially acceptable alternate form of sexual release for adults, whether or not one has an active partner.

Alcohol consumption prior to the sexual act is a major cause of sexual performance failure.

Sex educational materials may also be introduced for the purpose of: (a) desensitization to previously taboo thoughts and behaviors; (b) technique learning; (c) increasing eroticism; and (d) increasing ability for sexual fantasy. Couples may be sent into the field to view X-rated movies or read books such as *Joy of Sex* (Comfort, 1972) and *Total Sex* (Otto & Otto, 1972). Couples generally experience an exhilarating sense of naughty intrigue with such assignments. Their responses to these materials are explored and used to establish sexual exercise goals.

Increasing Eroticism and Fantasy Life

Increasing erotic fantasies facilitates increased sexual frequency. In a study involving two weeks of sexual fantasy practice and training for men aged 45-55, there was a mean increase of 42% in their rate of erectile response and a 34% increase in their rate of intercourse (Solnick, 1977). Furthermore, erotic literature and self-generated fantasies were particularly effective stimuli for increasing erectile response.

Although a rich fantasy life is vital to healthy sexuality many husbands and wives are so absorbed in daily routine that their sexual fantasy life is virtually nil. The wife may need help to integrate increased, explicit sex fantasies with her self-ideal. In other words, to understand that a woman can dream about and enjoy sex and still be a lady!

Couples write in explicit detail and share their ideal sexual fantasy involving their partner before body contact exercises are introduced. Frequently the wife's fantasy reflects a strong need for more romantic and tender behaviors while the husband's fantasy reflects specific sex act desires. Sharing this information can lead each to fantasize how best to meet the other's affectional and sexual needs–to the ultimate benefit of both. To increase both sexual fantasies and sexual interest one or both partners may be given a reading program of erotic literature.

Selected Sexual Exercises and Pleasure Communication

Couples frequently avoid normal body contact because any touch is misinterpreted as a sexual overture. Couples are taught to enjoy both giving and receiving nurturant caresses, and to communicate sexual desires directly to increase intimacy and to avoid misunderstanding or limiting affection.

Sexual pleasuring exercises, foot and head caressing, or sensual body massage may be introduced to develop greater body involvement and expand sensual pleasure (Masters & Johnson, 1970; Harman & Fithian, 1974; Graber & Graber, 1975). Partners learn to express directly, and without embarrassment or anxiety, their sexual needs which may not agree with normative data. They learn to become verbally and nonverbally expressive during sex to guide the partner's pleasure-giving ability. Mutually agreed-upon exercises proceed slowly under patient control in order to prevent anxiety or negative emotional response.

Technique Changes to Minimize Effects of Aging in the Male

Although the aging female does not experience much change in sexual capacity, both partners must understand changes in the aging male and adjust their sexual patterns accordingly, in order to minimize the effects of these changes and to be left feeling mutually satisfied. A common-sense approach to sex is required that involves alternate non-demand pleasuring of each other, and removal of the "touchdown mentality" requiring end-product orgasm. Couples are taught to be lighthearted and to enjoy each sexual encounter for whatever it brings.

Since older females can remain multiply orgasmic, the elderly male can learn to enjoy love play without the ultimate goal of orgasm for himself. If he is not competitive with his wife and is secure in his own sexuality, he can find pleasure and stimulation in helping her achieve her capacity for orgasm. Problems of loss of ejaculatory inevitability or of erection can be avoided by teaching the male to have an orgasm when he feels like it and then to continue pleasuring the female. This approach is psychologically better than concentrating on maintaining the erection and losing it.

Older males may require more intense direct stimulation of the genital region to obtain erection and ejaculation. The female must understand that this need is not a reflection of her lessening physical attractiveness to stimulate her mate but part of the male aging process. The male may also need direct hand stimulation of the genitalia during intercourse for ejaculation to occur, and must communicate this need. Frequently the wife must be trained to be a more active participant in the sex act. This can at first be highly threatening to couples with narrowly defined, stereotyped sex roles, but they can be helped to accept this as their attitudes become freer.

A frequently encountered sexual problem in older males is premature ejaculation. The Victorian attitude coloring their sex education, that a "lady" did not enjoy sex and that a "considerate" husband made intercourse as brief as possible, enhanced frigidity in females while conditioning poor sexual techniques and inducing premature ejaculation in men. If the male can be taught to enjoy prolonged high levels of sexual tension instead of just orgasmic gratification, premature ejaculation can be eliminated.

Sexual Growth

As stated initially, some couples on this program who follow these procedures have developed an increase in sexuality that exceeds their earlier age activity. For example, one husband aged 62, in a new sexual atmosphere of playful unhurriedness now consistently has two orgasms per sexual session when his prior lifelong pattern involved only one orgasm per session (Sviland,1975b). It had simply never occured to him that satisfactory sex could lead to more satisfactory sex at the same time. A few other couples in their mid-sixties now average four to six orgasms per week while one male aged 64, over a six-month timespan, twice exhibited only a 10-minute refractory period between orgasms.

These results belie current statistical data. However, this is not too surprising, in light of the wide gap that exists between sexual potential and the average sexual performance on which data are based. Couples who have shown sexual growth on the program appear to employ the following factors of sexual enhancement: (1) mutual lovingness and physical attractiveness; (2) increased sexual desire through enhanced fantasy life; (3) frequent practice effect; (4) playful, leisurely atmosphere blocking performance anxiety; and (5) enthusiasm positively reinforcing the partner's efforts.

In summation, this program has successfully changed behaviors and attitudes within weeks. Sexual therapy directed to helping elderly couples become sexually liberated not only has positive social vlue but has enabled elderly couples to open mutual communication, to increase intimacy and self-esteem, and to enjoy without guilt the sexual pleasures that society restricts to its youth. More such services to elderly couples should be provided.

References

Alberti, R. E. & Emmons, M. L. *Your perfect right.* San Luis Obispo, Ca: Impact, 1974.

Annon, J. *The behavioral treatment of sexual problems* Volume I. *Brief therapy.* Honolulu: Kapiolani Health Services, 1974.

Berezin, M. S. Sex and old age: A review of the literature. *Journal of Geriatric Psychiatry,* 1969, *2,* 131-149.

Berne, E. *Games people play: The psychology of human relationships.* New York: Grove Press, 1964.

Butler, R. N. *Why survive? Being old in America.* New York: Harper & Row, 1975. (a)

Butler, R. N. Psychiatry and psychology of the middle-aged. In
A. M. Freedman, H. I. Kaplan & B. J. Sadock (Eds.), *Compre-
hensive Textbook of Psychiatry/II.* Baltimore, Williams &
Wilkins, 1975, 2390-2404. (b)

Christenson, C. V. & Gagnon, J. H. Sexual behavior in a group of
older women. *Journal of Gerontology,* 1966, *20*(3), 351-356.

Claman, A. D. Introduction to panel discussion: sexual difficulties
after 50. *Canadian Medical Association Journal,* 1966, *94,* 207.

Comfort, A. *Joy of sex.* New York: Crown, 1972.

Davies, L. J. Attitudes toward old age and aging as shown by
humor. *Gerontologist,* 1977, *17*(3), 220-226.

Dean, S. R. Sin and senior citizens. *Journal of the American
Geriatrics Society,* 1966, *14,* 935-938.

Dean, S. R. Sexual behavior in middle life. *American Journal of
Psychiatry,* 1972, *128,* 1267.

Feigenbaum, E. M., Lowenthal, M. F. & Trier, M. L. A report of a
a study. *Geriatric Focus,* 1967, *5*(20), 2.

Fensterheim, H. & Baer, J. *Don't say yes when you want to say no.*
New York: Dell Publishing, 1975.

Graber, G. & Graber, B. *Woman's orgasm. A guide to sexual
satisfaction.* Indianapolis: Bobbs-Merrill Co., 1975.

Hartman, W. E. & Fithian, M. A. *The treatment of sexual
dysfunction. A bio-psycho-social approach.* New York: Jason
Aronson, 1974.

Kaplan, H. S. *The new sex therapy.* New York: Brunner Mazel,
1974.

Kassel, V. Polygamy after 60. *Geriatrics,* 1966, *21,* 214-218.

Kassell, V. You never outgrow your need for sex. Presented at 53rd
Annual Meeting New England Hospital Assembly, Boston
(March 27, 1974).

Kinsey, A; Pomeroy, W. B. & Martin, C. I. *Sexual behavior in the
human male.* Philadelphia: W. B. Saunders, 1948.

Masters, W. H. & Johnson, V. E. *Human sexual response.* Boston:
Little, Brown & Co., 1966.

Masters, W. H. & Johnson, V. Human sexual inadequacy. Boston:
Little, Brown & Co., 1970.

Newman, G. & Nichols, C. R. Sexual activities and attitudes in
older persons. *Journal of the American Medical Association,*
1960, *173,* 33-35.

Otto, H. A. & Otto, R. *Total sex.* New York: New American Library,
1973.

Pfeiffer, E. & Davis, G. C. Determinants of sexual behavior in
middle and old age. *Journal of the American Geriatrics
Society,* 1972, *20,* 151-158.

Richman, J. The foolishness and wisdom of age: Attitudes toward the elderly as reflected in jokes. *Gerontologist,* 1977, *17*(3), 210-219.

Schaie, K. W. & Strother, C. R. Cognitive and personality variables in college graduates of advanced age. In G. A. Tallend (Ed.), *Human behavior and aging.* New York: Academic Press, 1968.

Solnick, R. L. Alteration of human male erectile responsiveness and sexual behavior. Unpublished doctoral dissertation University of Southern California, 1977.

Stokes, W. R. Sexual functioning in the aging male. *Geriatrics,* 1951, *6,* 304-308.

Swartz, D. The urologist's view. Panel discussion, Sexual difficulties after 50. *Canadian Medical Association Journal,* 1966, *94,* 213-214.

Sviland, M. A. P. Helping elderly couples become sexually liberated: Psycho-social issues. *Journal of Counseling Psychology,* 1975, *1*(5), 67-72. (a)

Sviland, M. A. P. Sexual rejuvenation in men over 60 — and women too!: Sexual therapy techniques. Workshop presented at Recent Advances in Sexual Research, Third Annual Western Meeting, The Society for the Scientific Study of Sex. Los Angeles (September 19, 1975) (b).

Sviland, M. A. P. Helping elderly couples attain sexual liberation and growth, *SIECUS Report,* 1976, *4*(6), 3-4.

Sviland, M. A. P. The new sex education and the aging. In H. A. Otto (Ed.), *The new sex education.* New York: Association Press. (In press).

Verwoerdt, A., Pfeiffer, E. & Wang, H. S. Sexual behavior in senescense. II. Patterns of sexual activity and interest. *Geriatrics,* 1969, *24,* 137-154.

The Experiential Approach in Learning about Sexuality in the Aged

Helen Elena Monea

"I am a lonely, withdrawn lump—
seldom approached—seldom cared for."

The above statement was the experience of one of the participants in an experiential workshop. They used clay as a medium to portray the feelings of an aged person disabled through some major illness that afflicts the aged. The workshop was part of a two day conference dealing with the theme of sexuality and the aged. Speakers and participants dealt with the idea that senior citizens had a need for sexual expression, that there was a need to assist the elderly in acknowledging and enhancing their sexuality, and that the elderly had diminishing ability to become actively involved. Generally there was a mood and attitude of optimism relating to sexuality in the aged. There was no discussion during the first day of the conference about the aged who would not consider sexuality as one of their needs.

Participants who selected my workshop in health factors and sexuality experienced the depression and loneliness of an aged, handicapped person with no desire or interest in sexuality. They used clay to express themselves as handi-

115

capped elderly. A variety of shapes, feelings and attitudes emerged. Depression, loneliness, and being a non-individual were major themes. Sexuality was the lowest priority. The participant who sculpted half a man, representing a stroke patient with no interest in sexuality, commented that patients had the right to initiate the topic of sexual concerns rather than the nurse, doctor, or friend. Another participant who shaped her clay in a flat abstract form symbolized her difficulty in talking about sexuality. The theme of trust emerged and was discussed in relation to interventions with the aged and the need for privacy and confidentiality. Their concerns were not congruent with the positive attitude of the morning conferences. I had expected the sexual theme to be the main consideration of the participants and that the clay would bring further considerations of sexual concerns related to impaired health. Therefore, I was surprised when the topic of sexuality was farthest from their minds and instead, the feelings of depression were prominent. If participants had selected a less debilitating disease, sexual needs might have been the focus.

The next day of the conference, Dr. Isadore Rossman, a physician skilled in caring for disabled aged, emphasized the diminishing sexual needs of the aged, particularly in the disabled aged. He subsequently validated what the participants using clay had experienced as the reality of the disabled aged. Therefore, themes developed by the group through the experiential workshop are pertinent to consider in patient care. In assessing patients' needs, it is crucial that we understand what they as individuals need, and not generalize or assume that their needs are like any other aged person. It also is important to develop a trusting relationship with the patients so that they feel safe in expressing their needs and to acknowledge the patient's right to privacy, choice to discuss, and confidentiality. Staff members need to be sensitive communicators with an ability to use discretion. If the ill aged use up their energy on depression and loneliness, priority should be focused on helping lift their depression and loneliness. Only then, perhaps, can they have energy for life experiences.

Experiential Learning

Using clay as a medium for communication allows for more authentic expression of thinking and feeling by reducing the defenses. The approach can be described as experiential, for it opens the path to the feelings behind cognitive learning. The affective domain of learning is experienced through aligning feelings with intellectual thoughts. Subsequently, a comprehensive dimension of learning that incorporates the affective and cognitive domain evolves. I have used this approach on an individual and group basis in teaching, consultation, and counseling and find that it continually enhances communication and learning. I learned the approach through teaching with Patricia Pothier, R.N., M.S., University of California, and have had opportunities to integrate it into gerontological nursing education through the opportunities offered by Irene Mortenson Burnside, R.N., M.S., private consultant and author in gerontology.

A brief description highlighting the experiential structured media experience is followed by theories and concepts related to the four phases of the process, i.e., body relaxation, mental imagery, multi-media, and sharing. Two of my students close the paper with their experiences in teaching/learning.

The Media Experience

Ideally, six to ten people allow for more intimate sharing. However, the approach can be modified for large groups provided there are qualified assistants. The leader plans the experience according to the level of development, personality, and age of the participants. Guidelines to insure optimal learning include precautions so participants and/or leader are not unduly overwhelmed with the experience. Recommendations include appropriate timing of the experience, giving participants choices of being actively involved or observing, choice of stopping the experience, choice of sharing or not sharing, and observing participants for anxiety reactions. The selection of a medium depends upon the goal of the experience. For instance, the use of art supplies to make a collage of a world together explores group growth, and the use of movement may be used for increasing body awareness. In preparing a plan that is based on the use of clay as the medium the leader needs to be particularly cautious since clay allows for quicker and more in-depth emotions to occur.

The purpose for the use of structured media experience is to increase self-awareness and ego-enhancement. After a series of meetings, the focus can then be developed toward expanding toward interpersonal awareness. To reduce anxiety, I make a statement at the beginning of the session to clarify and reassure the participants that the goal is not to have a group therapy, sensitivity, or T-group experience, but to learn more about what one's own attitudes and feelings are about a current topic such as sexuality and the aged. They are given a choice to participate or observe. If they choose to observe, they are asked for feedback about what they observed and experienced.

The most favorable setting is a well-lighted room with privacy and sufficient floor space to form a circle of pillows and blankets for sitting. A bucket of water and paper towels for washing hands after the work with clay should be available. The clay can be offered in a large bag for the whole group or placed in individual paper bags for each participant. I prefer having the learners select their own clay because it gives them a choice of how much they need. Participants quickly become involved and preoccupied in handling the clay; therefore, instructions need to be clear that the clay is not to be worked until directions are given.

A short period of body awareness is introduced in which the participants are encouraged to close their eyes and concentrate on relaxing their bodies. With eyes closed, they are asked to fantasize themselves as an aged person or an aged person they know. They are encouraged to visualize what they are wearing as an aged person, what type of illness they have, such as diabetes, cancer, or senility. To help them further increase the awareness of the aged self, they are asked to concentrate on how the professionals taking care of them respond to their illness. . .how their family responds. . .how a close companion, wife or husband responds—and then how the illness affects their sexuality. The final direction is to shape the clay in the form of their experience with their illness and sexuality.

When they complete their clay sculpture, they are directed to slowly open their eyes and look at their sculpture. Using newsprint and felt tip pen, they describe their clay sculpture. Partners are then selected to share the experience for ten minutes, comparing similarities and differences in their sculptures. Some partners choose to meet in adjoining rooms or in the hallway while others remain in the classroom. The purpose of sharing with partners is to give the participants an opportunity to verbalize on a one-to-one basis and become acquainted before the group discussion. Sharing as partners and in the group, provides an opportunity for further integration. For instance, a participant may make a connection of an idea or express a feeling that was not fully developed in the one-to-one discussion. Comments from group members often act as catalysts in furthering the expression of feelings while expanding the discussion. The group process is one of sharing, and not necessarily confronting, so participants have the opportunity to explore their own attitudes and feelings.

Sharing in a group is sometimes threatening; therefore, participants are given a choice of sharing only what they are comfortable in sharing. This choice reduces the anxiety that might result from group pressure to share, and therefore minimizes resistance. The opportunity of choice also protects the participant who may reveal too much and then feel anxious, guilty, and/or angry.

The experience is meaningful for most participants, depending upon what their experience and attitudes are about innovative ways of learning, their personality, and what is going on in their lives at the time. Occasionally some participants feel that they have not understood or gained anything from the experience. These statements often mean resistance for a variety of reasons. Aside from the reasons already mentioned, there is the possibility that the participant may have become too involved and the leader may not have intervened at the right time, or the intervention may not have been helpful. Often the learning takes place after the participant distances from the experience and the participant is unaware of what he or she has learned. It is important for the leader to allow for the expression of the resentment without becoming defensive. The leader needs to be alert to any anxiety reactions such as tears, changes in breathing or swallowing, paleness or giggling. Knowing when a participant is becoming too involved and intervening appropriately is a skill developed through experiencing the process oneself and working with all ages. For the aged, use comfortable chairs and a table instead of pillows on the floor. A reminiscing-group experience which assists the elderly to share and integrate their past with their present could be enhanced by the use of structured media experience.

Theories and Concepts Related to Experiential Learning

Science has found that the two sides of the brain coincide with two different functions; the logical or cognitive with the left side of the brain and the intuitive and creative with the right side (Ornstein, 1972). Traditional learning has focused on the left side leaving the right side to chance development (Hendricks and Fadiman, 1975). Transpersonal education, human learning and experiential learning are similar in that they focus on enhancing the abilities and potentials in the right side of the brain. My own approach is eclectic, and, includes Eastern/Western philosophies and methods. The basic pattern in my experiential sessions is (1) body relaxation, (2) mental imagery, (3) use of media for self-expression, and (4) sharing the experience.

Body Relaxation. The first goal is to help the participants reduce tension in the body and quiet the mind so the two can function as a unit. It is a well-known fact that the body and mind influence each other. If the body is tense, the mind is not relaxed; conversely, if the mind is tense, the anxiety will appear in some fashion such as tapping fingers on the table, fiddling with an article, or looking pale. Concentrating on relaxing the body can reduce the heart rate, blood pressure, and metabolism (Benson, 1976). Biofeedback is another method of training people to control blood pressure and prevent migraine headaches (Brown, 1974). Gestalt therapy has similar concepts; it encompasses the whole person including what the individual is thinking, feeling, and doing. Awareness of these three entities promotes self-understanding.

Participants and observers often comment about the soothing and calming effect my voice has on them during the relaxation and imagery experiences. The importance of the leader's voice enhances or detracts from the creative experience. Using a quiet tone, speaking clearly and slowly, adds to the quiet serenity of the atmosphere needed for optimal relaxation. Timing the directions at adequate intervals requires sensitivity to participants' body language (Monea, 1976). I modify my approach for people who have sensory losses, as in older adults, by positioning myself closer to them, keeping their eyes open, or using a microphone.

The therapeutic quality of the voice has been successful in healing through a technique called toning (Keyes, 1973). The tone of the person's voice can indicate the state of mental or physical health. People with whiny or sucking sounds, for instance, have been identified by Keyes as having negative health conditions. They cling to problems or illness since it gains attention and importance in their life. Reversing their tone of voice can change their state of health. People learn how to heal themselves or others through toning by producing sounds in rhythm with the body (Keyes, 1973).

Mental Imagery. Researchers have found that body relaxation facilitates the flow of internal images (Richardson, 1969). The use of mental imagery is used to intensify the experience and leads participants into the inner self where they ponder upon a suggested scene, memory, object, or experience.

Historically, imagery has been used for healing from ancient times until the present. Today, tribes such as Canadian Eskimo and the Navahos of the American Southwest have *shamans*, who use their special powers of visualization for healing. In ancient times, Egyptians, Orientals, and East Indians evolved a mode of healing based on people experiencing visualization themselves (Samuels & Samuels, 1975). Today, Simington, a radiologist, assists cancer patients to battle the cancer by visualizing their cancer cells being attacked by their white blood cells. Some of the patients have experienced spontaneous remission (Bolen, 1973). Therapists use autogenic training developed by Dr. Schultze forty years ago; this involves relaxation and visualization of a specific problematic part of the body being either warm or cold. The method has been extensively researched with successful reports in many patients and is used a great deal in Europe (Luthe, 1969). Many American professionals today are incorporating the approach.

Medicine is not alone in using visualization. Healing the mind through visualization has been used by psychology. Freud and Jung found that bringing images to the surface of awareness could make a person feel better and grow emotionally. Freud used the process of free association related to conflicts while Jung used the free imagination of letting images come to mind (Samuels & Samuels, 1975). Contemporary therapists such as behavior therapists use visualization to reduce anxiety about specific fears by desensitizing the person through gradually increasing the visual images of the object of anxiety. Hypnosis, guided affective imagery and psychosynthesis are other methods that use visualization for healing the mind (Samuels & Samuels, 1975).

Meditation, a means of achieving psychological quiet, originated from Eastern cultures. People who have practiced methods of meditation have already developed skill in concentration and relaxation that is useful in visualization (Samuels & Samuels, 1975). I find students who are skilled in yoga and/or meditation are able to immediately enter a relaxed state, develop rich imagery, and are less resistant to new experiences of learning.

Research indicates that working with imagery can have a beneficial effect on physical, emotional, and mental aspects of life. If students have access to these tools, they can be used for continual growth throughout their lives (Hendricks & Fadiman, 1975). The movement of expanding our consciousness in these other directions of learning is influencing academic education. Concerned teachers, administrators, and parents are supporting and introducing new techniques for optimal learning in the classroom (Hendricks & Roberts, 1977).

Multi-Media. Using a form of media such as clay, drawings or montage materials allows for symbolic expression of the visualization experience, giving the participants an opportunity to test out and explore their own unique way of creating. Creativity and healing are different, although both arrive from the process of visualization through the reverie state (Green, 1971). Developing the creativity of professionals is an important aspect in improving the quality of care of the aged. The creative process has been described by Wallis as having four stages (Patrick, 1955);

1. *Preparation:* Data is collected in the mood of perplexity and excitement.
2. *Incubation:* The critical stage where ideas are mulled over by the unconscious while the person is directing attention elsewhere.
3. *Illumination:* This stage brings spontaneous solution or inspiration usually accompanied by feelings of certainty and joy.
4. *Verification or revision* is the last stage in which the person consciously plans the idea.

The above process has been experienced by students as they begin to use the media to transform their visualization experience into a symbol. However, the critical stage does not seem to take long and their attention is present throughout.

The principles of art therapy as described by Rhyne are congruent with the goals of experiential learning (1973). Participants are assured that the use of media is not for artistic expression but a self-journey for expressing their own attitudes, beliefs, and feelings about sexuality and aging. Otherwise students strive for artistic work in competition with others, while some feel inadequate in the use of art media. In experiential learning, the leader's role is not one of therapist. No interpretation is done. Instead, careful listening to the participant's experience and what it means to him or her is appropriate. Although internal conflicts may be alluded to or shared, no interpretation follows except for skillful support and guidance in sharing or keeping silent. Sometimes peers interpret a participant's work; this can be misleading and cause defensive reactions. The leader can comment on the distinction between individual internal differences in perceptions and experiences.

Sharing. Another way of integrating the experiences is through sharing media expressions with one person, then the total group. Talking with someone often illuminates and clarifies perceptions. Support and validation of their own perceptions or the sharing of opposite viewpoints can be a beginning to changing attitudes. The topic of sexuality for some groups is intimidating and anxiety-producing. Often, strong values, attitudes and beliefs and sharing polarizes differences. Since the goal is not therapy, the leader needs to acknowledge that participants should only share what they are comfortable with, and that they may choose not to share at all. The statement reduces the anxiety for those who feel the group pressure to talk. For some people, the topic of sexuality has been taboo, especially in talking about sex with a group of strangers. For further guidelines see references (Monea, 1976; Monea, 1978).

Learning How to Teach Experientially

The University of Hawaii Summer Institute in Gerontology gave me an opportunity to offer an intensive two-week course in teaching experientially. The first week was focused on learning theories, concepts, and experiencing the group process. The second week, students worked with partners to create and implement lesson plans with their peers as participants. The learning and creativity was a peak experience for many students and myself. Two highly competent students led their peers through an experience in an area of sexuality that is often overlooked. Their approach was unique because (1) the topic of sexuality was based on a broad definition, and (2) they used three different media for integration that helped their classmates safely relate with each other and themselves. May I introduce you to two special and talented people: Kate Cogeshall Hammat, former Recreation Director, Pullman Convalescent Center, Pullman, Washington, and Jeannette C. Takamura, Director, University of Hawaii Health Team Development Program and Instructor, Schools of Medicine and Social Work.

I. Introduction

When we considered the development and implementation of a lesson plan for a class session on sexuality and aging, we were aware of the many facets of the topic to which we could address our efforts.

However, our combined work experiences were rich with compelling memories of incidents which illustrated the confusion, embarrassment, and frequent avoidance of the issue of the sexual and intimacy needs of the elderly by families, professional staff, and the aging themselves. No one we knew had escaped the struggle with personal and sometimes tenaciously held biases regarding sexuality and the elderly. In many instances, it appeared to us that the many myths associated with aging and sexuality were being perpetuated by those in contact with the elderly out of ignorance, frustration, and fear.

In settings such as convalescent centers, we saw human sexual needs barred by de-personalizing physical environments and silenced by unspoken codes of social conduct. We observed, not only in the microcosmic worlds of such settings, but also in the supposedly empathic and caring environs of family homes, that many elderly with sexual and intimacy needs were cast as perverted, giggled about, scorned, or pitied. Sadly, we also found many of the aging filled with guilt and shame about their sexual feelings as a result of their own acceptance of uninformed community views and attitudes. Painfully subjected to society's insensitivity or tired resentment of their needs, among them the need to love and be loved and to receive and give human contact, the elderly we knew responded by withdrawing, regressing, becoming more aggressive, or by exhibiting themselves.

However convincing the arguments for the building of knowledge and understanding about the sexual and intimacy needs of the elderly, we anticipated the reticence of some students to becoming involved in the study of a traditionally sensitive topic. As a result, we decided to trust our experiences and, for the purposes of the class session, to use a broad definition of sexuality. In addition to familiarizing our classmates with the physical and pyschological factors which affect the sexual functioning and activity of the aging, we also encouraged them to explore sexuality in the context of the relationship and intimacy needs of the elderly. An outline of the lesson plan developed appears on page 127.

II. Students' Responses

Photographs. One of the students commented that she had discovered the tremendous amount of warmth and sensitivity which a friend had for her. Another woman, who had brought a picture which showed her husband, son, and grandson, said, "I used to be very dependent, have hurt feelings, and feel rejected. I feel that I have found new ways of showing how *I* care. So much of intimacy and of really relating depends on my own identity, my own self-perception." All of the students were able, through the mental imagery related to their photographs, to identify the most cherished aspects of their significant relationships. Several of our classmates stated that they hoped that equally deep and meaningful relationships will continue to be theirs even in their later years.

Montage. In explaining what her portion of the montage said about the message society gives us about sexuality, one student shared, "EVERYTHING has sexual connotations! Cars, perfumes, glamorous women." Other students observed that elderly men were always paired with bright, younger women, that women were being cued to strive for youth, that homosexuality is made to seem the rage or an outrage, and that men are pushed to be MEN.

All the students seemed in agreement that our society tends to present highly glossed pictures and messages which suggest that popularity, "goodness", sexuality is anything that is young, vivacious, kinky, and shiny.

Clay. As students watched and listened to one another share their clay pieces, many of them seemed to have *satori* experiences. Placed on the montage, which encircled the photographs, the clay sculptures suggested a harsh dissimilarity between what society has said is desirable and what the students envisioned themselves wanting as elderly. One student noted, *"Why, it's so simple; it's all there, isn't it? What we want has nothing to do with glitter and glamour. It's that intimate relationship that counts."*

The sculptures included one that resembled the palm of a hand. According to the student-creator, the palm supported and cared. Another sculptor molded two clay figures close together and explained that companionship would be important to her in what she anticipated would be her tranquil period of life. Throught their sharing, the students in our class seemed to be indicating that sexuality is more than just two individuals having intercourse. The interactional process and intimate giving and receiving were recognized as significant, nurturing human needs.

III. Experiences in Planning and Implementing the Lesson Plan.

Although we had little difficulty planning and implementing our lesson plan, there are several points which we feel were given special thought and attention. Throughout our preparation, we were aware of the importance of our making conscious use of ourselves, our bodies, our voices, our energy, and our movements as we led the class. We made a special attempt to determine how we assessed our own teaching strengths and our own preferences for portions of the didactic and experiential content. We were also critically conscious of our use of time and timing. Finally, we made explicit our need for assistance from one another during various segments of the session.

Thanks to Helen's very expert role-modeling and to her encouragement that we be creative, we had a rewarding and enlightening time learning even more about sexuality, intimacy, and aging.

Lesson Plan: SEXUALITY AND INTIMACY

I. INTRODUCTION

    A. Objectives.

    By the end of the class session, the student will be able to:

        1. Identify physical and psychosocial factors which affect sexual functioning and activity among the aging,

2. Describe human intimacy and relationship needs regardless of age,
3. Describe the special intimacy and relationship needs of the elderly,
4. Discuss sexuality and aging in the context of relationship and intimacy needs,
5. Compare society's views on sexuality and aging with the student's personal views.

B. Overview.

Students were provided with an overview of some of the current concerns of gerontologists with regard to aging and sexuality. Students were also provided with the research conclusions reached by Masters and Johnson in their study of the sexual responses of a population of elderly persons. Much time was given to an elaboration of the common isolation, alienation, and loneliness experiences among the aging; their unrelenting losses, and their social relationship needs in comparison to other age groups.

II. BODY RELAXATION

Students were instructed to settle into comfortable, unlocked positions and to slowly close their eyes. The class was reminded that each person was being entrusted with the responsibility of monitoring and assessing her readiness for progressive participation throughout the mental imagery exercises. Students were instructed to become aware of their breathing, to let themselves experience a sense of relaxation, and to focus in on and relax tense points in their bodies.

III. MENTAL IMAGERY

A. Mental Imagery Related to Photographs

Each student has been asked to bring or to draw a picture of someone whom she loved. The instructors suggested that the student(s):

1. Recall a happy time she shared with her special person,

2. See what this special person contributes to her sense of well-being and happiness and vice versa,

3. Recall a happy time when they experienced physical closeness and caring, and if she felt free enough and if it were appropriate, to imagine an experience in which there was sexual intimacy,

4. Recall her own feelings and her observations of her special person's feelings of the happy time when physical closeness and caring were shared.

B. Mental Imagery Related to Collage (Montage) Making

The instructors asked the student(s) to:

1. Imagine herself as an aged person,

2. See what she looks like, moves like, feels like as an aged person,

3. Observe what the world says about sex and sexuality. Think about what is said over the television, through the papers, at cocktail parties.

C. Mental Imagery Related to Clay Sculpturing

The instructors asked the student(s) to:

1. See what she looks like, moves like, feels like as an aged person,

2. Bring in her special person and see what she wants to give and get as an aged woman,

3. See what's so about what she'd like in their relationship,

4. See what's so about sexuality.

IV. MEDIA AND SHARING

A. Photographs.

After the mental imagery exercise, each student was asked to share whatever was meaningful and comfortable about what she learned about the special person in her photograph. The photo was then placed in the center of a large (5' X 5') sheet of white paper (on the floor).

B. Collage.

Following the collage mental imagery process, the students were instructed to work individually on a collage which depicted what society suggests are essential for anyone to be sexy or to achieve an intimate relationship.

C. Clay.

After completing the imagery exercise which accompanies the clay sculpturing activity, the students were given clay and instructed to create some form which communicated what they had experienced.

Summary

The experiential approaches described in this paper are some of many avenues being developed and explored in innovative methods to increase learning about oneself and the aged. If you try the experiential approach, Kate, Jeanette and I welcome you to the exciting and rewarding experience of learning, teaching, and/or counseling creatively.

References

Benson, H. The relaxation response (5th reprint). New York: Avon, 1976.

Bolen, J. Meditation and psychotherapy in the treatment of cancer. *Psychic,* July, 1973.

Brown, B. *New mind, new body: Biofeedback; New directions for the mind.* New York: Harper & Row, 1974.

Green, E. Speech at De Anza College, Cupertino, California, 1971.

Hendricks, G., & Fadiman, J. (Eds.). *Transpersonal education: A curriculum for feeling and being.* Englewood Cliffs, New Jersey: Prentice-Hall, 1975.

Hendricks, G., & Roberts, T. B. *The second centering book: More awareness activities for children, parents, and teachers.* Englewood Cliffs, New Jersey: Prentice-Hall, 1977.

Keyes, L. E. *Toning: The creative power of the voice.* Marina del Rey, California: DeVorss, 1973.

Luthe, W. *Autogenic therapy.* Vol. I. New York: Grune & Stratton, 1969.

Monea, H. E. *Instructor's Manual, Nursing and the Aged* (Irene M. Burnside, Ed.) New York: McGraw-Hill, 1976.

Monea, H. E. Experiential teaching: Its use in group work. In I. M. Burnside (Ed.), *Working with the elderly: Group process and techniques.* North Scituate, Massachusetts: Duxbury, 1978.

Ornstein, R. E. *The psychology of consciousness.* San Francisco: W. H. Freeman, 1972.

Patrick, C. *What is creative thinking?* New York: Philosophical Library, 1955.

Rhyne, J. *The Gestalt art experience.* Monterey, California: Brookes/Cole, 1973.

Richardson, A. *Mental imagery.* New York: Springer, 1969.

Samuels, M., and Samuels, N. *Seeing with the mind's eye: The history, techniques, and uses of visualization.* New York: Random House; Berkeley, California: The Bookworks, 1975.

Sexuality and Aging: Implications for Nurses and Other Helping Professionals

IO

Bernita M. Steffl

Introduction

This chapter is devoted to issues and problems that confront health professionals who work with older adults in community settings, acute hospitals, and long term care facilities.

Though we have made progress in the past five years, there are still those of us who need to get better educated about human sexuality across the life span and examine our own feelings and attitudes toward sexuality in the aged.

There are still professionals who do not understand that the "dirty old man" and the "shameless old lady" may be the healthiest old people while they go about locking the feelings, hopes, dreams and fantasies of these individuals in the cage of age. What's more, we may be locking ourselves in that cage via a self-fulfilling prophecy. We can liberate them and ourselves. "They are us" (Eisdorfer, 1977).

In our society we have developed a rather negative attitude to the whole process of aging and toward the aged, so it is not strange that we have rather stereotyped notions about sex in the old. Some of these are:

1. Old people do not have sexual desires
2. They could not make love if they wanted to
3. They are too fragile physically and it might hurt them
4. They are physically unattractive, therefore sexually undesirable
5. The whole notion is shameful and decidedly perverse. (Butler & Lewis, 1977)

Even though most of us could not as children and cannot even now comfortably imagine or accept the notion that our parents are interested in or indulge in sex, we are learning that the same hopes, dreams, feelings, desires, and passions we had in youth remain within us! The same "me" of 10, 20, and 30 years ago is still locked in the body with some of the same desires of yesteryear, and old age is always in the distant future. Even when we are 60 and 70, old age is 10 years hence!!

In working with older people it is becoming increasingly clear that sex is a major concern in late life. In my experience with older people, I have noticed much more preoccupation with sex and sexuality since I have become more aware of their basic human needs and since I have sharpened my listening and assessment skills. Fear about loss of sexual prowess is a common preoccupation for the older man and can reach devastating proportions; "Old ladies do not sit on park benches just to watch the children play . . . they dream of their lovers and their lover's lovers."[1]

Sex and Medical, Surgical, and Chronic Physical Conditions

Sex complicates things for doctors. Sex histories on medical records are usually nil. A good medical history and physical should include a sex history. Not all the blame for avoiding this topic belongs to doctors, though they are guilty and probably are still perceived as the most significant source of help by patients. Psychologists and psychiatrists have paid the most attention. However, nurses, social workers, and other professionals should not avoid the topic just because the medical doctor has.

Arthritis

In chronic conditions sex can be both therapeutic and preventive. For example there is some evidence that sex activity helps arthritis even in severe arthritic patients, probably because of the adrenal gland production of cortisone and because the sexual act itself is a form of physical activity. Also, emotional stress can result from sexual dissatisfaction, and stress worsens arthritis; so sexual activity can be helpful in maintaining function (Butler & Lewis, 1976).

Sex After Hysterectomy

To many women the uterus is not only a child-bearing organ but also a sexual organ, a cleansing instrument, a regulator of general body health and well-being, and a source of strength, youth and feminine attractiveness. Thus, counseling for post-hysterectomy sexuality is apt to be much more involved than sometimes anticipated. For example, we often hear women complain about the weight gain, feelings of weakness, fragility, and vulnerability; phrases such as: "I feel an emptiness, a space here in my stomach," or, "Something is missing and I eat so much to try to fill up the emptiness" (Drellich, 1967, p. 62).

There should be no problem having sex after hysterectomy. The vagina and female barrel are intact and there is ample room for penile penetration. Numerous studies have shown that loss of ovarian hormone has virtually no effect on sexual desire, sexual performance, or sexual response. When disturbances do occur, the physician is best equipped to handle problems (or should be if he is interested). These disturbances to sex life are not uniform but are related in most instances to irrational fears and psychological effects of surgery in the genital area (Drellich, 1967).

Common Gynecological Problems of the Aged

A persistent theme in geriatric medicine has been the reticence of many elderly patients to complain about serious physical problems. This is especially true in relation to gynecological problems in the female and prostate problems in the male. Because early detection has a direct relationship to recovery, everyone should have regular physical examinations and direct questions should be asked by doctors and nurses. The most prevalent gynecological problems are:

Senile vaginitis, vulvitis, and peritoneal pruritis. All of these are low-grade inflammations which cause a great deal of discomfort and itching. They are caused by hormonal deficiencies, vitamin deficiency, sugar in the urine, poor hygiene, allergies, or invasion of organisms from the rectum or outside the body (equipment or clothing). Symptomatic treatment with cleansing douches, cornstarch, and topical medications are most helpful. These conditions are very persistent and take strict routine care; the very old and disoriented patient may need special attention and understanding. As stated earlier, hormonal creams and water-soluble lubricants may be helpful.

Uterine prolapse. Prolapse of the uterus means a downward displacement. It is measured by degrees. In a third degree prolapse the uterus descends to the point of hanging out of the vagina. It is suspended by stretched uterine ligaments. A prolapsed uterus can be manipulated into place but descends again as soon as the patient stands up. Surgery is the treatment of choice, but may be contra-indicated by the patient's age or general condition. In older patients a Gellhorn or doughnut type pessary may be inserted to hold the uterus in the pelvis. These must be replaced frequently and require extreme cleanliness; care must be taken that they do not cause ulceration or become misplaced (Durbin, 1968). Because older women are fearful, too embarrassed, or too senile to complain, we unfortunately see more of these conditions than we should in large custodial care settings. We can do something about these problems and should consider counseling and educating families of aged patients about them.

Cystocele and rectocele. These are prolapses of the bladder and the rectum which, when severe, can cause problems in voiding and bowel elimination. With the cystocele or a urethrocele the patient may dribble urine, compounding the problem; in most cases surgical intervention alleviates the problem; however, again these are conditions the elderly woman hesitates to report until it is a major problem.

Finally, the everlasting catheters that are so commonly used for incontinent patients in nursing homes are a major vehicle for introducing bladder infections, and sometimes lead to serious problems. First, the writer believes that too often an indwelling catheter is the too simple solution, and that we get lax about taking them out because bladder retraining for the elderly is not easy; secondly, most extended care facilities claim they do not have the help to keep patients dry when they are totally incontinent. I can only say that I believe a catheter should be used only as a last resort.

Prostatectomy

Prostate problems and prostatectomy are so prevalent that we must spend some time on these. In my own experience I have learned that an appalling number of misconceptions exists.

Although the operation is widespread, many men and their wives have only a hazy idea of the prostate's function and why its strategic location can cause distress. The prostate is made up of muscular and glandular tissue and is located just below the urinary bladder. The urethra, the tube that empties the bladder, passes through it. The sole function of the prostate is to produce a fluid to transport sperm cells during sex relations.

As men grow older, the urethral glands that lie inside the prostate often grow bigger. The enlarged prostate can then press on the urethral tube and block the outlet of the bladder. This leads to stoppage of urine and sometimes serious consequences to the kidneys. Usually surgery is recommended when a man has a diminished stream of urine and/or difficulty starting the stream.

There are several popular methods of doing this surgery, and urologists will select the best method for the particular patient and his problem. I have found:

1.   Patients are rarely counseled by the doctor about sex life after prostatectomy. When they are, it is not very thorough. Two things happen: (a) "You'll soon be good as new," or (b) "Well, George, what do you expect at your age?"

2. The surgery is usually worse than expected. The tubes, the blood in the urine, and the general discomfort are worse and more complicated than the patient was led to believe.
3. Sexual dysfunction may take place, but does not necessarily need to be permanent. Patients need to be educated what to expect and encouraged to expect a return of sexual function.

Procedures commonly used in prostate surgery do not disturb the innervation of the erectile system and only rarely result in impotence (about 5%). In most patients postoperative impotence is of psychogenic origin, particularly in the case of older men who are convinced that the need for the operation confirms his senescence. Though the procedure does not interfere with erection and ejaculatory sensation, it does often produce sterility. This is obviously important for the young man or older man who is married to a younger wife and plans to have children (Basso, 1977). Because of the removal of obstructive portions of the prostate, the basic structure of the bladder neck is changed and usually then after surgery the semen is discharged, not forward through the penis, but backward into the bladder. The sensation and climax (orgasm) of intercourse are the same and no harm is done in this "retrograde ejaculation." The semen then issues forth with the next passage of urine. It must be emphasized that this has nothing to do with obtaining erection (Daut, 1974).

Nurses are in strategic position with patients to supplement or initiate this kind of patient education and should be prepared to do so. If they are uncomfortable in doing so, they should still be able to assess the situation and seek out other members of the health team to assist them.

Impotence

"Impotency" and "sterility" are often used interchangeably by clients. They may need help in understanding that impotence does not imply sterility. Impotence may be complete or partial, temporary or permanent. A male may be completely impotent with one woman and not another. Potency depends upon two sets of factors, one being organic and the other psychological. It is important to say here that nurses and health professionals should understand the physiology of penile erection or seek help in doing so (Finkle and Thompson, 1972).

Myths of childhood about diseases have strong influence over older males in regard to impotency; these beliefs can become a self-fulfilling prophecy. Also, the ego of the aging male is especially vulnerable to rejection, either real or illusory.

Doctors Finkle and Thompson (1972) reported encouraging success in counseling 84 psychogenically impotent males. They suggest that for many such patients pragmatic counseling rather than extended psychotherapy will achieve renewal of satisfactory sexual function. Dr. Finkle also emphasizes the great importance of the physician's attitude, interest, and hope. With the positive and optimistic attitude of the physicians involved, 53% of the patients (N=84) responded satisfactorily to four or less visits.

Penile prostheses sometimes offer a satisfactory solution for the male whose impotency has been established as being organically based. One such prosthesis involves the insertion of semi-rigid lengths of silastic rods into the *corpus cavernosa* using surgical procedures (Pearman, 1972). A hydraulic device also is available. When erection is desired, the patient manipulates a subcutaneous pump and fluid is released into two cylindrical prostheses inside the *corpus cavernosa,* producing an erection. This is called the Scott-Bradley-Timm prosthesis (Basso, 1977). It is extremely important that before either one of these prostheses is used the male be interviewed to determine that he has a healthy sexual attitude, and that he understands what the operation can and cannot do for him.

Some men have reported that a hard, doughnut-shaped rubber device slipped over the partially-erect penis can be helpful in maintaining an erection. It fits tightly at the base, and retains blood in the penis necessary for erection. This device may be purchased in shops dealing in sexual materials. A leading marriage counselor once pointed out that a simple strong rubber band may serve the same purpose and be less expensive and less objectionable, so I tell my students, "If you see an elderly man with a rubber band around his penis, know there may be some 'method in his madness.' "

There are some local genital disorders that are often misunderstood and cause not only problems but a great deal of guilt and fear. One such condition in males is Peyronie's disease. Peyronie's disease in men can interfere with performance. Hard tumors form in the body of the penis and interfere with intercourse; the penis angles to the right or left. The etiology is unknown. It often disappears by itself in about 4 years. There are various treatments. Peyronie's disease is thought to be rare, but may be more common than we thought and could certainly cause psychological problems (Butler & Lewis, 1977).

Cardiovascular Conditions

Cerebrovascular accidents and coronary attacks are two of today's greatest fears. Some people believe that sexual activity may bring on an attack or cause a recurrence or even death. Attacks and deaths have occurred during sexual intercourse; however, good and conclusive data and statistics are not available. We do know that oxygen consumption in sexual intercourse is equal to climbing stairs or walking briskly and that the heart beat increases to 90-150 beats per minute (average 120).

Death during sex occurs much less frequently than people fear, though probably somewhat more often than reported due to reluctance to report — a conservative estimate is 1% of all sudden coronary deaths. I can validate this from my personal experience in working with older adults. Women have confided in me about how this happened to their husbands, and the problems they have had with their guilt. Most of them indicated they would have liked more post-coronary counseling about sex.

Generalized findings of researchers indicate that, with any type of heart disease, the patient who can comfortably climb one or two flights of stairs or take a brisk walk around the block is ready to resume sexual activity — usually 4-5 weeks after heart attack, providing there are no complications. Researchers believe that sexual intercourse should be denied only for those patients in severe congestive heart failure, and even for those, other sexual activities involving stroking, touching, and embracing are possible (Scheingold & Wagner, 1974).

Strokes

Strokes (cerebrovascular accidents) do not necessitate cessation of sexual activity. It is very unlikely that further strokes can be produced through sexual intercourse. If paralysis occurs after stroke, adaptations in sexual positions may be necessary to compensate for weaknesses (Butler & Lewis, 1976).

Parkinson's Disease

Parkinsonism or *paralysis agitans* is commonly known as "the shaking palsy." It is a progressive, debilitating disease with characteristic tremors, shuffling gait, masked expression, and depression. The disease affects twice as many men as women, and has a late onset. Working with and communicating with the Parkinson patient is very difficult for most of us; perhaps it is because of our own feeling helplessness to reverse what we see happening. Although these patients often maintain cognitive function, the patient's lack of affect and difficulty in communicating fosters alienation by nurses. Assessing for his sexual needs is very unlikely; however, we should be aware that fostering social and sexual interest may be helpful. Levadopa (Bendopa, Dopar), the medication often used in treatment of Parkinsonism, is one of few medications that crosses the blood-brain barrier. Studies have demonstrated that, in addition to lessening tremors and relieving depression, it may enhance libido and activate sexual behavior in a small number of patients. Nurses working with these patients should be aware of opportunities to counsel and assist the patients and their spouses for sexual intimacy when and if possible (Costello, 1975).

Ways to Resume Sexual Activity After Illness

The person who is in good physical condition and who engages in regular exercise will be in better condition physically and emotionally to resume and enjoy sexual activity after cardiac problems or any illness.

Masturbation, for those who find it acceptable, is a good way to ease back to normal sexual activity. The cardiac cost is substantially less for both men and women than sexual intercourse. The individual can find out if he or she is still sexually responsive, and thus gain confidence when sexual activity with a partner is resumed.

Increasing sanction is given to masturbation these days as professionals are working out their "hang-ups" and acceptance. However, they may forget to take the patient through this stage. For example, a very attractive and spunky older widow participating in a discussion on this subject, said "Our sexuality is talked about, written about; they wonder — do we? And they say what is bad and what is good for us — widows like me. Masturbation always comes up, but nobody tells us exactly what it is, how you do it, or where you do it!"

There are very specific suggestions and precautions for post-coronary patients which also apply to other conditions. Warning signs of heart strain include rapid heart and respiratory rate persisting 20-30 minutes after intercourse, palpitations continuing 15 minutes after intercourse, chest pain during or after intercourse, sleeplessness following sexual activity, and extreme fatigue on the day following intercourse.

When to Avoid Relations

It is best to avoid sexual relations under the following conditions:

1. Immediately after a large meal or drinking alcohol
2. If environmental temperatures are extremely cold or hot, especially when weather is hot and humid, because of physiologic demands to maintain body temperatures
3. If the situation is anxiety provoking, or if negative feelings or anger or resentment exist between partners.
4. If strenuous activity is anticipated after intercourse.

Variation in Positions for Intercourse

Intercourse may be less stressful if the coronary patient assumes the on-bottom position. Although current research shows some measurements of physical exertion are not significantly different in the on-bottom and on-top positions, the increased isometric muscular activity in the arms and shoulders and the increased peripheral resistance occurring in the on-top positions are thought to be more demanding on the heart. Because findings are inconclusive, a more passive sexual position is recommended for the coronary patient. The patient is advised to lie on his back during intercourse with his partner kneeling so that he does not bear weight.

An alternate position is to sit on an armless chair with his partner sitting on his lap. The chair must be low enough so that both partners touch the floor with their feet. A side-lying position is also recommended and may work very well for some (Puksta, 1977).

Organic Brain Syndrome

Because of their impaired cognitive functioning and consequent poor judgment and poor impulse control, patients with organic brain deterioration may exhibit sexual behavior that is inappropriate with regard to time, place, and social context. Examples are exhibitionism (the flasher), masturbation in public, and pedophilia. These behavior manifestations of dementia may occur among geriatric patients in long term care facilities and are usually very upsetting to personnel, patients and families (Verwoerdt, 1976). Nurses, other health professionals, and paraprofessionals often do not realize that they may provoke the very behavior that upsets them; that is, they often provoke behavior with comments like, "How's my boyfriend today? Are we going out tonight?" Then, when the patient with assumptions based on a fake relationship makes familiar advances, he is chastised and the nurse becomes upset. This can be very traumatizing and confusing to the disoriented patient. I hope this does not imply that we should not be warm and friendly with these patients. They desperately need our touch, love, and affection. But we must give it in such a way that the confused patient knows the limits and where he stands. Working with this kind of patient requires a fixed routine and consistent reality orientation to time, place, and person with a network of redundancy cues.

Sexual Acting-Out

Patients may express hostile or rebellious tendencies through provocative sex acts such as exposing genitalia. Patients also learn through some sort of conditioning that certain behaviors (such as wiggling out of bed clothes, soiling self or attacking others) brings about opportunity to be touched. Disturbing sexual behavior may be a manifestation of confusion, anger, loneliness, or boredom. Too often this patient is punished instead of being loved and is then pushed further into his well of loneliness and depression.

Aphrodisiacs

One cannot discuss this subject without touching on man's (and woman's) search for eternal youth. The search and various remedies have existed for centuries. Even today intelligent men and women, young and old, attempt to enhance sex and their sexual conquests and abilities with "hallucinogenic drugs" and "aphrodisiacs." Males tend toward this search more for the obvious reasons just discussed.

Older individuals are not as apt to try hallucinogenic drugs as foods and other aphrodisiacs. "Spanish Fly" (*Cantharidis*) and amyl nitrate are two of the most common. All men should be cautioned that these are not really aphrodisiac, but are truly dangerous. With Spanish Fly, the action actually irritates the lining of the genitourinary tract as it is being excreted; the irritations may produce sensations resembling sexual arousal, bringing about genital urge and a reflex erection. It is a powerful corrosive poison and can cause tissue destruction.

More recently amyl nitrate has gained popularity. The aficionados claim this substance enhances the intensity and pleasure of orgasm. This drug is a vasodilator which is sometimes used to relieve *angina pectoris* victims. Theoretically, the drug, which is "popped" during the height of sexual arousal, may act by increasing the vascular response of the genital organs. There is no scientific data to prove that it is aphrodisiac in this way, but *it is medically dangerous.* Coronary occlusions, some resulting in death, have been reported to follow the use of amyl nitrate during intercourse

(Kaplan, 1974). Some of my students tell me that popping amyl nitrate is currently very popular among homosexuals.

There is not room here to discuss the aphrodisiac claims laid to many foods and vitamins. My personal philosophy is: if it is not destructive and the individual feels that it helps, why not?

Drugs and Sexuality

Drugs and alcohol are usually more inhibitory than aphrodisiac. They may release behavior temporarily from inhibition in small doses, but large amounts depress all human behavior, including sex, and chronic abuse of sedatives seems to generally diminish human sexuality (Kaplan, 1974).

Drugs may affect various aspects of sexual behavior. Some alter the libido or intensity of sexual interest and pleasure, while others affect only the physiological response of the genitals: erection, orgasm, and ejaculation. Unfortunately, most drugs or substances which influence human sexuality diminish rather than enhance erotic pleasure.

There are several mechanisms by which drugs can influence sexuality. Essentially this involves a chemical alteration of the nerves which regulate the sexual response. Some drugs act primarily on the brain by altering function of the sex centers. These can enhance or diminish libido. Other types of medication influence the peripheral nerves which regulate the functioning of the sex organs. Still another mechanism is alteration of response of the genital blood vessels. Some chemicals modify sexual behavior directly; others produce secondary changes. Drugs differ in that they may act discretely and affect only the sexual response or they may cause general toxic conditions which carry with it changes in sexuality.

Assessment of drug effects is complicated because drug action is complex and depends on so many variables. In general, the effects of drugs on male sexuality are far better documented and understood than is their influence on responses of females. This is partly due to the fact that the male response is more visible and quantifiable: for example, erection is easier to assess and study than orgasm. To list and/or discuss the effects of the various categories of drugs which may have an effect on sexuality is impossible here, but I will emphasize three points:

1. There is no drug without some effect
2. Professionals should include questions and information on drugs when taking a sex history
3. Clients should be sure to report what drugs they are taking or have taken

Sexercise

To my knowledge Bonnie Prudden (1961) was the first to set forth in print fundamental exercises every normal man and woman can practice in order to enjoy a full, happy, and vital sex life. She states that we can do specific exercises to stay physically fit for sex just as athletes do certain exercises to remain fit for tennis or football. Since sex takes physical expression along with mental and spiritual expression, it seems logical that we keep those muscles needed in shape.

Sexercises will also improve the appearance of the body. An attractive body is only one of the prerequisites for more pleasurable and meaningful lovemaking. Another is the ability to make that body function as it can and should. "If you set out to develop your sex muscles with exercise, you can for the most part keep them in shape with daily sports. If, however, you don't care for sports, but do like to make love, then it's the exercises ten minutes a day for the rest of your life" (Prudden, 1961, p. 144).

Space here does not permit me to describe and diagram the sexercises that Bonnie Prudden recommends. I would suggest that professionals in counseling roles purchase her book, *How to Keep Slender and Fit After Thirty,* and suggest it to clients who are interested and apt to follow up on physical fitness routines.

Following is a list of specific sexercises which are described and pictured in the book:

Gluteal Exercise
Pelvic Tilt: standing, sitting, supine, etc.
Pelvic Tilt: walking
Seat Lift
Hip Swing
Stretch Outs

Circle Tilts
Leg Lifts, Weighted Leg Lifts
Head to Instep Exercise
Crotch Stretch

It should be noted that very little goes on in life without benefit of the pelvis. Every exercise for the pelvis also improves posture and guards against backaches. "There is no question but that the best lover is the one with whom we are in love. But how much better it is if the partner has a highly trained body. A Beethoven sonata will always sound better on a concert piano than a kazoo" (Prudden, 1961, p. 159).

In late years many women develop weakened pelvic muscles which makes them feel the vagina is losing its ability to grip the penis. The Kegel exercises for women are specific for this problem. The Kegel exercises consist of 20 to 30 contractions of the muscles of the pelvic floor, as though holding back from urinating and defacating at the same time. These exercises should be performed several times daily and can be done while working, sitting or standing. Contractions are held only a few seconds and the process must be repeated at least 100 times a day to be truly effective. The Kegel exercise also helps to maintain support of the pelvic structure, the uterus, bladder, and rectum (Butler & Lewis, 1976). The *Sana Session* (Treber, 1976) also contains sexercises.

What to Teach Old People

We can start by teaching the older person that sex can last into the later years. It is more than emotional and communicative. It is learned rather than instinctive and can be developed by anyone willing to try. Love and sex are always there to be rediscovered. Older people have time! And experience counts! Sex does not merely exist after 60; it holds the possibility of becoming greater. It can be joyful, creative, and a happy healthy giving. It is morally right and virtuous. It unites human beings (Butler & Lewis, 1976).

Anxiety about coital performance can be lessened if we teach old people that there are a variety of ways besides direct genital contact by which the partner can gain satisfaction, such as digital manipulation of pressure points, oral stimulation, and masturbation. The use of vibrators should be discussed, and those who are comfortable with the idea of using them should be encouraged to do so. Most older people are not ignorant or unaware of the depth of human sexuality, but they often are naive about terminology and harbor misconceptions and taboos from their early training which we can help them liberate. Contrary to expectations, older individuals are not hesitant to discuss sexuality, particularly their own. It is usually the professional who has problems approaching the subject.

I have found older individuals respond when I use a very factual, professional approach, sometimes with a little humor to ease anxiety. They seem to expect me to be informed, and respect my opinions and/or advice. I always express my own belief — that sex is a very personal and private affair, but that this does not make it a taboo topic. I also like to emphasize that expressing our sexuality helps us maintain a sense of self, a sense of identity, and a means of self-assertion that feels good.

In counseling and in health care, it is important to take a sex history. Masters and Johnson (1970) suggest a list of topics to cover. During interviews or in care settings the nurse or other professionals in the helping role should observe for messages through body language and listen for feelings: listen with the third ear for what the patient did not say. Books on general physical fitness, *Sex After Sixty* by Butler and Lewis and *Joy of Sex* by Comfort, should be recommended to patients. They can be especially helpful to couples when the therapist goes over questions with them after the reading. Other information to teach patients is discussed in other sections of this chapter.

Sexuality and the Institutionalized Elderly

This topic is covered in more detail in other chapters in this book; however, everything I have said here should apply to nursing home patients as well as elderly persons in the community. If not, I'm sure you are as aware, as I am, that it is probably because nursing homes are geared more to needs and desires of families and smooth institutional operation than desires of the patient. The above, and the fact that most nursing home patients are usually without spouse and somewhat or totally immobile, makes any kind of social-ization (let alone sexual gratification) somewhat of a challenge.

However, since sexuality includes much more than intercourse there are many opportunities for the alert, sensitive and motivated professional to provide enhancement of basic human needs for nursing home patients. Following are some question guidelines for improving the plight of nursing home patients concerning sexuality:

1. If there is a problem related to sex, ask: With whom is the problem? Patient? Staff? Family? What can I do about it?

2. Are physical problems related to sexuality such as senile vaginitis, catheters, etc. well taken care of in your institution?

3. Are you helping staff examine the meaning of the behavior of "the dirty old man" and "the shameless old woman?"

4. Are you aware of the isolation and sensory deprivation of the immobile patient?

Can you:

5. Provide more touch, hugging, kissing, hand holding, and intimacy such as back rubs and body message?

6. Build sexuality into (rather than separate) the spiritual and emotional well-being of your patients?

7. Accept and allow masturbation and help your staff deal with it?

8. Provide more touching and feeling things to handle, fondle, and hold, such as yarn balls, prayer beads, and stuffed animals?

9. Bring live pets into your setting and allow patients to feel and cuddle them?

10. Provide more music: romantic, sentimental, sen-suous, erotic?

11. Encourage opportunities for sexes to meet, mingle, and spend time together, such as in small television rooms, without structuring a "trysting time or place" too rigidly?

12. Provide double beds for married couples?

13. Counsel families, particularly adult children of patients, about sexual needs of older people?

14. Manipulate the environment to make your facility a therapeutic milieu?

And finally:

15. Do staff and patients laugh (and maybe cry) together?
16. Do you have a Bill of Rights for sexual freedom in your facility?

Counseling Guidelines for Professionals

Old people do seek counseling on sexuality and sexual concerns, but we don't always hear them and most of us are not well enough prepared to help them. Successful and continuing sexual activity is but one sign of healthy aging. Following are some pointers and guidelines to assist those who are working with older individuals who may need sexual counseling.

I. Communication Skills

1. Examine awareness of your own beliefs, values, and attitudes toward aging and the aged and sexuality.
2. Assess interpersonal skills necessary to:
   a. Initiate communication with the elderly
   b. Create atmosphere conducive to discussion of sexual concerns
   c. Listen for nonverbal cues of sexual concerns
   d. Elicit verbalization of underlying concerns
3. Review knowledge of sexual physiology and functioning.
4. Assess client's perception of his/her sexual concerns.
5. Ask yourself, "What kind of nonverbal messages am *I* sending?"

II. Helps In Assessing the Problem.

1. Is the problem a request for information about anatomy and physiology?
2. Is the need a specific sexual problem?
3. Is the problem a clinical situation directly or indirectly related to sexual functioning?
4. Is the problem organic or situational requiring alterations in preferred mode of functioning?

5. Is it a crisis or a long term problem?
6. Is the person trying to live up to some preconceived performance expectations and creating his/her guilt for failure? The "Inner Ball Game" may be interfering with the real game.
7. Assess for physical illness or disorders and medications.
8. Always look at what is left, not what is gone.

III. **Points of Departure For Initiating Discussion on Sexuality With Older Persons.**
   1. Consider or find out the client's early orientation to sexual behavior.
   2. Look for feelings (residual) about masturbation as a child, which still may be present unconsciously.
   3. The "first time" seems to have great significance, so consider it as a point of departure in discussion.
   4. "The second time around" is often described as being better, so one might use that as a point of departure for discussion.
   5. Tie sexual behavior and history in with other social activities, religion; and remember, it may take time to come around to the topic and questions or problems.
   6. Listen for a double message: "I don't think about that." "I would if I fell in love."
   7. Remember, there may be increased preoccupation (conscious or unconscious) with sexuality in old age, particularly in certain settings.
   8. Keep approach "confidential, private, personal."
   9. You don't have to know all the answers to counsel, you just need to help old people find their own answers, and sometimes they have them but need your sanction and or support.
   10. Avoid avoidance of the subject.

IV. **How Do You Limit Overt Sexual Exposure and Improper Advances?**
   1. Look at circumstances: night, fantasy, etc.
   2. Examine precipitating events.
   3. Look for need to prove masculinity or sexuality.

4. Assess for sensory deprivation.
5. Look for health in the situation; e.g., is man trying to prove something?
6. Recognize needs.
7. Recognize ability and need to live and function as man or woman?
8. Direct to a healthy outlet in appropriate place.
9. Do not punish.

V. How Do You Handle "The Dirty Old Man"?

1. Consider how you handle with your own peers. Young women may encourage similar behavior from a six foot football player and not expect to go to bed with him, but what makes it so "dirty" when an 80 year old, 100 pound man stares at her from the feet up, or reaches for her bosom? Anxieties like these are not easy to handle. They are the result of conflicts in a departure from our culture, our life style, and our comfortable cohort group. We may need help in handling them. Unfortunately, this help is usually sought after the fact; nevertheless, it helps to share experiences and do problem-solving as a team.

VI. How Shall We Deal With Masturbation?

1. Recognize it as acceptable and healthy.
2. Examine our own attitudes.
3. Certain aspects of sex are private; so is masturbation, so encourage proper time and place.
4. Do not punish or ridicule.

VII. Mechanical Stimulation

Whether counseling or simply educating older individuals, health and helping professionals should be informed about the availability, prevalence, and use of vibrators and other mechanical devices used to stimulate the genitalia and other erotic zones of the body. The use of various kinds of vibrators and intrusive devices is quite common; for example, an electric toothbrush has been used.

A nurse told me in confidence that when one of her aged nursing home patients was no longer able to masturbate, the administrator obtained a vibrator for her. No doubt personnel in institutions, especially those giving direct care to patients, could tell us much more about coping strategies and innovations, but our taboos have made it too dangerous for them to do so.

Conclusion

In conclusion, I am pleased to share the experience of a nurse. I do not know her, but hope that you and I will do as well in our work as she has.

> Two weeks ago as I made my hospital rounds, Mr. C extended his right hand and Mr. C with his left hand showed me his penis and stated, "I love you." I had a mental block and finally spoke to him in an understanding way, "You haven't had sex for a long time and this is a normal feeling." Mr. C slowly covered himself with the top sheet. The next day I visited Mr. C and told him of my concerns about his sexual behavior. I asked him if he would like to go on a pass if his wife could handle him. He answered, "Yes." I talked to the physician about Mr. C, and she left an order for a pass. The social worker made arrangements with Mrs. C for a pass on Father's Day via Handicab. Mrs. C was also offered the petting room, which she declined and giggled, remarking, "No, I'll take him home where he can touch me." This initial pass led to another weekend pass, and, I hope, many more passes. (Caringer, 1976)

References

Adelson, E. Frank talk about older sex. *Modern Maturity,* 1974, *17(1),* 48.

Basso, A. The prostate in the elderly male. *Hospital Practice, October 1977, pp. 117-123.*

Butler, R. W., & Lewis, M. I. *Sex after sixty.* New York: Harper & Row, 1976.

Butler, R. W., & Lewis, M. I. *Aging and mental health.* St. Louis: C. V. Mosby, 1977.

Caringer, B. *Sexuality in Aging.* Unpublished paper presented at the Maluhia Hospital, Honolulu, Hawaii, Spring 1976.

Comfort, Alex. *The joy of sex.* New York: Crown, 1972.

Costello, M. K. Sex, intimacy and aging. *American Journal of Nursing,* 1975, *75*(8), 1330-1332.

Daut, R. V. *So you're going to have a prostatectomy.* Norwich, N.Y.: Eaton Laboratories, 1974.

Drellich, M. G. Sex after hysterectomy. *Medical Aspects of Human Sexuality,* November 1967, pp. 62-64.

Durbin, M. S. Geriatric gynecology. *Nursing Clinics of North America,* 1968, *3*(2), 257-258.

Eisdorfer, C. *Mental health and aging.* Speech presented at the meeting of the Western Gerontological Society, Denver, March 1977.

Finkle, A. L., & Thompson, R. Urologic counseling in male sexual impotence. *Geriatrics,* December 1972, pp. 67-72.

Kaplan, H. S. *The new sex therapy.* New York: Bruner/Mazel, 1974.

Masters, W. H., & Johnson, V. E. *Human sexual inadequacy.* Boston: Little, Brown, 1970.

Prudden, B. *How to keep slender and fit after thirty.* New York: Random House, 1961.

Puksta, N. S. All about sex after a coronary. *American Journal of Nursing,* 1977, *77*(4), 602-605.

Scheingold, L. D., & Wagner, N. N. *Sound sex and the aging heart.* New York: Human Sciences Press, 1974.

Shumaker, S. Frank talk about older sex. *Modern Maturity,* 1974, *17*(2), 48.

Treber, G. J. *Sana session.* New York: Source Publishers, 1976.

Verwoerdt, A. *Clinical geripsychiatry.* Baltimore: Williams & Wilkins Co., 1976.

Footnotes

[1] I saw this quote on a poster some years ago. I am often reminded of it and am so sorry I cannot recall who said it.

Sexuality in ▌▌Nursing Homes

Mona Wasow and Martin B. Loeb

This is a report of a research project which grew out of the merging interest of two areas of concern of the problem-centered curriculum of the University of Wisconsin-Madison School of Social Work. Professor Wasow teaches problems in human sexuality and Professor Loeb teaches one of the courses in aging. The requirement of a research project led the seven students involved in this project to ask the two professors to supervise their research project on sexuality in nursing homes.

In reviewing the literature, we were able to discern three different areas of interest. The first is that of the potential for sexual activity throughout the life span. Masters and Johnson in particular, but also several others, have been able to convince us that, although there is a decrease in the potentiality for sexual activity as one ages, any cessation of this activity (given reasonable health) is likely to be social and psychological rather than biological. Based on this knowledge, there is another theme in the literature that discusses sexuality as being good for people, and from this theme emerges a series of "ought-to's." Thirdly, there is the area of empirical research, and one finds very little data of this type, especially data concerning institutions and nursing homes. That is what this project is about — what actually goes on in nursing homes. In order to do this study, we developed an interview schedule which has an open-ended, discussion-type question at the end — more about this later. The interview schedule covered four basic areas: attitudes, knowledge, actual sexual activity, and some demographic information. The main attitudinal areas we were concerned with were:

1. Sex as being primarily for procreation or recreation.
2. A double standard for men and women.
3. Who should be allowed sex; e.g. old people, teens, mentally ill, retarded, homosexuals, unmarried?
4. Is masturbation normal or not; good or bad?
5. Did the persons interviewed see today's mores as different from when they were young, and if so, how did they view them?

When looking at the respondents' actual knowledge, some of the things we were looking for were, for example:

1. What they knew about sexual potentials of elderly people; e.g., can women enjoy sex after menopause; as a man ages, does it take him longer to get an erection?
2. What did they know about masturbation?

When looking at sexual activity we asked three main questions:

1. How often do you participate in sexual intercourse, masturbation, sexual thoughts or fantasy?
2. If you are no longer sexually active, what reasons led to your giving it up?
3. Do you feel sexually attractive at this point in your life?

The interviewers were all young, and we had a training program for them in the areas of interviewing skills, aging, and sexuality. We interviewed both residents of nursing homes and a small sample of the staff in nursing homes. We tried to get an even age distribution in five age categories — 60-69, 70-74, 75-79, 80-84, and 85 and older. In all, we interviewed 27 male residents, 35 female residents, and 17

staff members, only one of whom was male. You will notice
in Tables 1 and 2 that the sample is primarily at the older end
of the age distribution for the residents, with the largest
proportion being over 85. Incidentally, there was twice the
proportion of never-married males to females.

Table 1

Number of Subjects Interviewed

	Number	Percent
Male residents	27	33
Female residents	36	46
Staff	17	21
Total	80	100

Table 2

Age Distribution of Residents (percent)

	Males	Females
60 – 64	8	0
65 – 69	15	14
70 – 74	4	11
75 – 79	19	17
80 – 84	19	30
85+	31	25
Not available	4	4
Total	100%	100%

We were struck by the fact that our sample showed that
25 percent of the female residents had some college and
about the same percentage had some professional experience
in their occupation. Both these figures for females (Table 3
and 4) are well over twice as great as found in the national
distribution.

Table 3

Educational Level of Residents (percent)

Education	Males	Females
1-8 grade	38.5	47.2
Some high school	15.4	13.9
H.S. degree	15.4	2.9
Some college	3.9	25.0
College degree	7.7	8.3
Graduate degree	11.5	0.0
Vocational school	0.0	2.8
Not available	7.7	0.0
Total	100.0%	100.0%

Table 4

Occupational Level of Residents (percent)

Occupation	Males	Females
Professional	19.2	27.8
Managerial	3.9	0.0
White collar	0.0	5.6
Farmer	11.5	0.0
Blue collar	50.0	30.6
Service worker	11.5	5.6
Homemaker	0.0	30.6
Not available	3.9	0.0
Total	100.0%	100.0%

This may not be surprising as we did a lot of the interviewing within a 25 mile radius of the University, though it also seems to hold true for the interviews held at a large northern rural nursing home. More than anything else, this reflects the way in which residents selected themselves to be interviewed. In many of the nursing homes, the staff asked residents whether they would be willing to be interviewed about sex. The staff told us that about 50 percent refused. In the large rural nursing home where our interviewers spent several days, they met refusals again and reported this at the level of 50 percent. Parenthetically, we are all going to hear of this kind of sampling distortion because of federal regulation controlling the use of human subjects.

The empirical findings about what goes on in nursing homes sexually can be seen at three different levels. First, there is actual sexuality, both dyadic and solo. Four women and two men claimed to participate in sexual intercourse and said they did this less than once a month. Three males and three females said that they masturbated. No area of questioning evoked as much discomfort, embarrassment, and denial as this one. For this reason, plus what the literature tells us about masturbation (that probably close to 100% of the population masturbates at one time or another), we doubt the accuracy of our data on masturbation. At another level of functioning there is the interest in sexual activity. Again, 31 percent of the males and 17 percent of the females still feel sexually attractive. (Table 5).

Table 5

Feelings of Sexual Attractiveness (percent)

Attractive?	Males	Females
Yes	30.8	16.7
No	57.7	77.8
Other	11.5	5.5
Total	100.0%	100.0%

In Table 6, it is shown that the reasons for being no longer sexually active are poor health (16 percent) compared to the 30-40 percent response of "no partner." It would appear that 40 percent of the females would be sexually active if there were an active partner available. Only 10 percent of the males, but 30 percent of the females said they lost all interest.

Table 6

Reasons No Longer Sexually Active (percent)

Reasons	Males	Females
Poor health	16.7	16.3
Lost interest	10.0	27.9
Not appropriate	6.7	7.0
No partner	30.0	39.5
Inability to perform	16.7	0.0
Celibate	6.7	7.0
No answer	13.3	2.3
Total	100.0%	100.0%

Still at another level of activity, that of fantasy, the data were mixed. Seventy-five percent of the women claimed none, but only 31 percent of the males claimed none. However, in interviewing with the open-ended question, we found (Table 7) many residents ascribing to other people in the nursing home a great deal of fantasy about sexuality. Statements would be made like, "No, I *never* think about such things! But Mrs. Jones down the hall . . . That's all she ever thinks about." Either every nursing home keeps its big fantasizer down the hall, or a lot of projecting is going on.

Table 7

Participation in Sexual Fantasy (percent)

	Males	Females
No	30.8	75.0
Yes	61.5	22.2
No answer	7.7	2.8
Total	100.0%	100.0%

One major analysis of the data that we performed was to correlate the attitudes that these residents had to sexual activity and the knowledge they had of facts about sexual activity. The sexual attitudes were derived through a review of the total interview by a panel of the researchers, and their judgments were tested through inter-rater reliability. The attitudes were categorized as permissive, semi-restrictive, and restrictive, and the factual knowledge was categorized into percent of correct answers. The correlation is clear; those with a very low factual knowledge (Table 8) were much more restrictive than those with high factual knowledge. This correlation was highly significant.

Table 8

Correlation of Respondents' Sexual Attitude and Knowledge of Facts about Sex*

Factual knowledge % correct	Permissive	Semi-restrictive	Restrictive
0 – 20%	3.6%	18.5%	45.8%
21 – 40%	7.1%	37.0%	29.2%
41 – 60%	57.1%	33.3%	25.0%
61 – 80%	32.1%	11.1%	0.0%
81 – 100%	0.0%	0.0%	0.0%
Total	100.0%	100.0%	100.0%

*X^2 = .001

There is an additional sex-related correlation with attitude. As might be expected, the highest proportion of female residents (47 percent) was considered to have a restrictive attitude. Male residents were almost evenly divided among the three attitudinal categories. On the other hand, the staff clearly had a more permissive attitude than did the residents. (Table 9).

Table 9

General Sexual Attitude of Respondents (percent)

	Male Residents	Female Residents	Staff
Permissive	36	22	65
Semi-Restrictive	36	31	35
Restrictive	28	47	0

It is not known, of course, that people would change their sexual attitudes if they were given additional factual information; perhaps some day we'll try that. One interesting and rather poignant finding of our young interviewers should be added. When they put their pencils and papers away, and asked the residents if they had any questions or further comments, they found a large number of people who really wanted some sex information. It really says something about our Victorian era when 80 year olds are asking: "Just what is a homosexual?" "Do normal people really masturbate?" Perhaps in many ways, we are still in the Victorian era; but that is another issue.

In summary, residents of nursing homes in general believe that sexual activity is appropriate for other people; however, most of them are not currently personally involved because of the lack of opportunity. Most of the respondents are spouseless. The staff of nursing homes are generally quite permissive in their attitudes about sexuality of older people, but we have no good information on what they actually do in specific situations. In one of the more generally permissive nursing homes we do know that an elderly man and woman escaped from the nursing home and got a room at a nearby motel. The staff found out about this and wanted to call the police to get the couple back. This brings up the problem of the difference between attitudes, and what people believe they have to do in order to maintain the decorum of the institution.

Elderly people in nursing homes *do* have sexual thoughts and feelings and indulge in some acting-out behaviors. Nursing home staff are frequently distressed and do not know just what to do. Sexuality of the aged has been one of the most neglected aspects of both the areas of aging and human sexuality. Traditionally we have viewed it as something that should not be there, and that if it is there it should be eliminated, controlled, and defeated. Perhaps a new day is coming, where we can learn to allow this pleasure to be available throughout the life span without shame and denial.

Sexual Practices and Administrative Policies in Long Term Care Institutions[1]

12

Dulcy B. Miller

Long term care institutions may be direct or indirect participants in a change in the American tradition of non-interference by government in the private lives of citizens. A good example of this appears in the Skilled Nursing Facility regulations published four years ago (Federal Register, 1974). By implication, moral and ethical determinants of behavior are proscribed in those regulations regarding patients' rights in nursing homes. The written words may appear innocuous, but they state that "a married patient in a long term care facility shall be assured privacy for visits by his or her spouse, and married inpatients may share a room unless medically contraindicated and so documented by the attending physician in the medical record . . . if a patient is found to be medically incapable of understanding these rights by his attending physician, such rights and responsibilities devolve to the patient's sponsor."

Perhaps the most encompassing statement is: ". . . the patient may associate and communicate privately with persons of his choice . . . unless medically contraindicated (as documented by his physician in the medical records)."

163

States are obliged to implement these federal regulations in their health codes. In this era of increasing emphasis on patients' rights, the administration of long term care institutions will need to develop policies regarding sexual practices of inpatients, including homosexual and heterosexual activity between brain-intact and/or brain-damaged residents.

A minimum of five possible courses of action exist:

1. The institution may adopt a hands-off policy, postulating that sex is a private matter to be determined by each resident for himself irrespective of his intellectual capacity, with no interference from administration.

2. A laissez-faire policy may be pursued where residents are encouraged to "do their own thing." Depending on the philosophy and the ethnic and social backgrounds of management personnel, this method will provide tacit, albeit passive encouragement or discouragement to sexual activities of inpatients.

3. The institution may act *in loco infantis.* If the latter course is followed, what must be ascertained are the wishes of the children of the resident in a nursing home regarding sexual activity. Families may differ, and siblings in one family may not share a single point of view. Children may feel differently about sex for their mothers than for their fathers.

    The long term care agency may actively encourage sexual fulfillment by patients as an important means of communication — as an activity to humanize the institution. If the goal for long term care patients is a full, rich life, it follows that sex among patients should be sought actively.

5. The nursing home may impose restraints on the sexual practices of residents in the belief that sex for the aged is unnatural and what is not natural is not good. Perhaps only certain publicly visible sex acts should be prohibited. Perhaps only senile patients should be protected from sexual involvement.

Implicit in the development of mature patient care and administrative policies regarding sexual experience of inpatients based on these five options is the realization that the long term care institution is affected by the attitudes of families, staff, volunteers, board members, professionals, and citizens in the community. Patient care and administrative policies must be formulated emphasizing the reaction of other patients to patient sexual experiences as well as the hostility, embarrassment, guilt, rejection, and compliance of the nursing staff and the families of patients. Appropriate administrative practices will surely be suggested by these groups.

Observations from the Literature

The literature regarding sex and well older individuals is extensive. Information relating to the ill aged and sexual activity in long term care institutions, however, is sparse and highly subjective.

In 1948, Kinsey, Pomeroy, and Martin noted that at age 60, 6% of the people were totally inactive sexually and by age 70, 30% were totally inactive sexually. In a 1959 study, the magazine *Sexology* noted that half of 102 men listed in *Who's Who* in the age groups between 75 and 92, questioned about their sexual practices, reported normal ejaculations, and 5% engaged in sex more than 8 times per month. A quarter of those interviewed masturbated and many had morning ejaculations.

In 1960, two physicians, G. Newman and C. R. Nichols, studied 250 blacks and whites between the ages of 60 and 93, noting that their sexual activity declined sharply after age 75. Blacks remained more active than whites, men more active than women; less affluent people appeared more active sexually than the wealthy. A full sex life in early years tended to continue into the later years of an individual, irrespective of color, sex, or economics.

In 1961, Dr. Joseph Freeman's studies in Philadelphia demonstrated that with men age 80, 22% experienced sexual desires but only 17% had sexual relations.

Dr. Destrem in France (de Beauvoir, 1972) noted that married workers were more active than their single counterparts and that the death of a partner frequently led to impotence on the part of the remaining spouse. Eric Pfeiffer (1968), while professor of psychiatry at Duke University, found no sexual limitation biologically for aging women but noted the scarcity of sexual outlets for unmarried women in their older years. Pfeiffer emphasized the importance of privacy for sexual activity.

A 1971 position paper by Dr. D. R. Mace emphasized that the maintenance of sexual capacity appeared to be closely related to the individual's own sense of identity and selfworth.

In 1973, Martin Berezin, a Boston psychiatrist, was reported in *Time* magazine as stating that institutions have become much more tolerant of sexual contact between unmarried residents, unlike the old days where those who wanted sex had to slip out into the woods like adolescents.

In April 1974, Dr. Alex Comfort, in an interview before the annual meeting of the American Geriatric Society in Toronto, commented that patients have constitutional rights to freedom of expression that are not forfeited when they enter an institution.

Mona Wasow and Martin Loeb (see Chapter 11) examined three levels of sexual activity in a group of nursing homes in the Madison, Wisconsin area. Dyadic and solo activity was reported by 22% of the study group, which represented approximately 50% of the population of the nursing homes in the study. Masturbation was reported by 11% with such discomfort that researchers believe the percentage was an underestimation of the number of institutionalized aged involved in this solitary activity. About 30% of the males and 17% of the females felt sexually attractive, and sexual inactivity was ascribed by 16% of the group to poor health and by 30-40% to lack of available partners. Of the males, only 10% had lost all interest in sex as compared to 31% of the females. The researchers felt that the 69% of the males and 25% of the females who reported sexual fantasies was an underestimation of the true number. A dichotomy appeared to exist in the expressed permissive attitude of the staff toward sex in the nursing home's population and what staff believed appropriate for the maintenance of decorum in the same nursing homes.

Norman Lobsenz in a 1974 *New York Times Magazine* article noted that in an era of more permissiveness toward sexual self-determination the puritanical attitude toward sex and the aged may be ascribed to oedipal fears and incest taboos associated with sex activity on the part of parental figures and thus all older persons as well as the cliches of a society which associates sex and beautiful youth. Lobsenz observed that society does not call a young person interested in sex a "dirty young man," but an older person with this interest is often described as a "dirty old man." The article characterizes the environment of the nursing home and home for the aged as desexualized, with privacy minimized by activities such as scheduled bed checks and hospital beds too narrow for satisfactory sexual activity. A Canadian physician mentioned in the same article had suggested the development of "petting rooms" in long term care facilities. The article further stated that doctors need to educate the aged concerning the sexual effects of medical problems.

Robert Butler, a noted psychiatrist and Director of the National Institute on Aging, commented that sex can be a therapeutic experience, citing the case of arthritics who can be helped by the increasing adrenaline gland output of cortisone as well as the reduction of psychological tension encouraged by the sex act. Butler noted that age permits sex to be viewed as an intimate activity — communication in its best sense. Further, he noted sexual activity offers institutionalized men the satisfaction of continuing masculinity and women continuing femininity, and affords both the sense of being wanted and needed, the comforting warmth of physical proximity, and the benefit of companionship and emotional intimacy.

Nature of the Patient Population in Homes

Some overall characteristics of the patient population to be found in the nursing home and home for the aged should provide a base for approaching policy considerations in the long term care facility. Females outnumber males four to one; most females are widows. Patients in the age group between the 75 to 85 decade predominate. Male patients are apt to present more severe disability; often their wives are living but were unable to cope with the nursing care needs of their husbands and placed them in an institution. Most ill aged women, on the other hand, have no spouse to care for them and may be admitted to long term care facilities less disabled than their male counterparts. Nursing home residents are ill physically, emotionally, or socially, or a combination of two or all three elements. Their average stay in the nursing home is two to three years.

The Physical Environment

Long term care institutions vary in size depending on their location, age, community needs, and sponsorship. Although the current average size is approximately 75 beds, newer facilities are considerably larger. Usually each facility contains more than one nursing unit; semi-private rooms predominate. Single rooms are infrequent in older nursing homes and are more prevalent in newer facilities. Federal and state regulations prohibit locks on doors in skilled nursing facilities, and beds must have siderails. Visiting generally occurs in patients' bedrooms following the pattern of hospital visitation or in general activity areas where families often engage in group visits. Occasionally specifically-assigned rooms are available in a nursing home for visits of a party character or for special occasions. Visiting sometimes takes place in garden areas in fair weather. Semi-private and multiple rooms always have curtains to assure privacy when the patient is being cared for by the nursing staff.

Philosophy and Program Goals of the Nursing Home

The goal of the skilled nursing care facility should be to encourage and help residents to function at their maximum level physically, socially, and emotionally. Improvement in function of the ill aged patient population is a slow and tedious process. The newly admitted patient more often than not is depressed and withdrawn. To help patients function at their optimal level it is essential to work with their families so that the institution and the family share realistic goals for the patient. Pre-existing family schisms may be manifested in the nursing home premises when families sabotage medical, nursing, and rehabilitation treatment programs.

Interested and Affected Individuals and Groups

Over a dozen groups of individuals may be identified as involved in some way with the subject of sexual activity in the institutional setting. They are listed here for consideration by the administrator:

1. Patients who engage in sexual activities
2. Other patients who do not
3. Families (children, other relatives, or spouses – male or female) of sexually active patients
4. Families of sexually inactive patients
5. Owners or board members who have the final responsibility for all institutional practices
6. Volunteers, including mature persons and impressionable candystripers aged 14 to 16.
7. Professional and non-professional staff, often presenting conflicting points of view
8. Visiting professionals, including physicians, social workers, and clergy, each with their own values concerning appropriate sexual practices for the ill aged in institutions.
9. Students such as interns, residents, nursing students who are present for clerkships or brief field trips
10. Friends of patients
11. Citizens in the community verbalizing concern for the quality of care in nursing homes
12. Government surveyors ascertaining fulfillment of federal and state laws
13. Voluntary agency personnel from the Joint Commission on Accreditation of Hospitals who conduct evaluations of the care program

On a recent television program, Irene Burnside, noted lecturer and author in health care and aging, said, "Let the residents be themselves in nursing homes." Being themselves means different things to different people. Each of the groups described above might have different expectations of residents, and might indeed behave differently sexually were they residents in nursing homes themselves.

Possible Range of Institutional Sexual Partners

Heterosexual activity may include a number of possible partners who may or may not reside in the institution:

1. A visiting spouse and brain-intact inpatient
2. Visiting spouse and brain-impaired inpatient
3. Married inpatients who are both brain-intact
4. Married inpatients where one partner mentally is intact and one intellectually impaired
5. Married inpatients where both are intellectually impaired
6. Married inpatient and non-spouse where one is intact and one is impaired
7. A visiting friend and non-spouse where the patient is intact
8. A visiting friend and non-spouse where the patient is impaired
9. Two inpatients who are not related and who are both intact
10. Two inpatients unrelated with one intact and one impaired
11. Two inpatients who are not related, and who are both impaired

Included in the possible range of partners in homosexual activities are:

1. A visiting friend and an intact patient who is married
2. A visiting friend and an intact patient who is unmarried
3. A visiting friend and an impaired patient who is married
4. Two intact residents, one married and one unmarried
5. Two intact residents who are both married
6. Two residents, one intact and one impaired, both unmarried
7. Two residents, one intact and one impaired, both married
8. Two residents, both impaired and both married
9. Two residents, both impaired and both unmarried

Because of the dearth and inaccessibility of partners for nursing home residents as shown above, one aspect to consider would be the amount of acceptance on the part of staff, relatives, etc., of solitary sexual experience, including masturbation.

Possible Range of Institutional Sexual Activities

Sex-related or associated activities include:

1. The question of turf, which may be of concern to the spouse of an inpatient who feels disturbed when a confused resident lies down in the bed of his spouse
2. Exhibitionism, with public exposure of genitals and other erotic areas
3. Fondling, either publicly or privately
4. Bedding together, not necessarily for sex but for the sense of human warmth

Administrative Implications: Areas of Consideration

Administrative implications of the variety of sexual and sex-related activities of the groupings described require careful consideration resulting in specific policies. In the instance of sexual activities among consenting brain-intact patients, perhaps the use of private rooms should be encouraged. Patients with visiting spouses or residents having relations with other persons in the institution in semi-private rooms are, in effect, imposing on the privacy of the other occupant of the room. Or, if private rooms prove economically unfeasible, long term care institutions may need to develop "sex therapy rooms," or waiting rooms for roommates. Perhaps the patient who wishes to engage in sex should be assigned to a specifically designated unit where staff are specially trained and sympathetic.

Since locks on doors are not feasible, should there be a special "Do Not Disturb" sign utilized to alert staff and other residents and visitors? In fairness to the other occupant of the semi-private room, should there be a time limit for the length of the visit for sexual activity? Should the practice of overnight guests in the nursing home be encouraged, and if so, should there be an extra wide bed in each room or should there by a special room available for overnight guests? Or should patients be encouraged to engage in off-premises sexual activities? Should the Basic Services Agreement include specific material concerning the responsibilities of the nursing home regarding sex? For example, if a patient has a living spouse, should the nursing home attest to the sponsor that his spouse will not be sexually active? Such policies will require special in-service education for the nurses and other staff regarding surveillance, appropriate methods of intrusion, etc.

The housekeeping department may need to schedule room cleaning around sexual practices; activity personnel, physical and occupational therapists and even volunteers might have to become involved in appropriate rescheduling. The medical director might wish to consider instituting a patient education program outlining sexual activity related to medical problems of the elderly and atrophy resulting from sexual disuse.

The Patient Care Policy Committee should consider the appropriateness of the width and height of institutional beds to accommodate two ill elderly people. A policy concerning the use of siderails during sex is imperative, for the institution probably will be responsible if the siderails are down and the patient or his visitor falls out of bed and breaks a hip. How such matters can be arranged with any degree of privacy for the participants is a challenge to institutional management.

Whose judgment should prevail when professional nurses determine patients are not physically able to participate in sexual activity against the express wishes of the patient? This brings up the question of patients' rights. The sexual activity of a patient with a catheter warrants exploration, as do the implications for infection control. For medico-legal reasons, nursing staff may wish to maintain a log of sexual experiences in the nursing home. A douche schedule should be developed to make certain that the ill aged, so susceptible to life-threatening infections, utilize proper hygienic methods. Are medical orders needed for sexual activity? Should nurses be taught to encourage solitary expressions of sexual activity? Should the nurses restrain the intellectually impaired so they will not attempt breast or genital caresses in a public or even in a private situation? Can nurses and other treating staff accept the notion that sexuality of the ill aged is healthful and not lecherous?

As part of the admission process, should the social work department elicit a sex history and a life style relating to sex? At admission the spouse or children should be required to give written permission concerning sex for the intact patient as well as for the intellectually impaired. Perhaps intact patients should state how they wish to be treated regarding sex should they lose their intellectual acuity. Before two people are placed in a room together, a commonality of attitudes toward sex should be ascertained. Certainly written permission from families for homosexual activity should be part of the admission process.

Undoubtedly the double standard, with families approving certain sexual activities at home but not approving the same activities in a public nursing home, will become evident. Families may feel differently regarding male and female parents engaging in sex; they may approve of sexual activity in male parents but highly disapprove of similar activity for their mothers. Thus, the possibility of disagreement between residents' wishes and family wishes regarding sex may be disruptive to all concerned, and may present a real dilemma to administration concerning whose wishes should be followed. Consumer advocates will quickly advise following the directives of the resident. Such advice is redolent of amateurism, for unless patient and family and institution agree, hostility, embarrassment, guilt, anger, and/or rejection will ensue.

Implications

In perspective, policies and procedures concerning the assignment of rooms and training of staff are simple in comparison to questions concerning the philosophy and implementation of a sex policy for the institution. Decisions will have to be made regarding the sense of order and decorum and regimentation. The rights of some patients for freedom and fulfillment of behavior should not be granted at the expense of other patients' freedom. The rights of the patients who disagree with sexual activity in the long term care unit merit attention, as do the rights of objecting families. The individuality of patients must be respected as long as other patients do not lose their individuality in the process.

Privacy for residents as espoused in the Federal Register may, in effect, prove non-existent when the mechanics for providing the opportunity for sexual activity publicizes the occurrence of this activity to other residents, staff, families, etc.

Administrative balance is essential. Group discussion with residents of two nursing homes revealed that sex is important to some patients, while others are indifferent to the issue and some are repulsed by the idea.

Simultaneously, administration must ascertain that societal inbred prejudice against sexual activity of the aged is not a determining factor in institutional policymaking. It is useful to recall that sexual restraint among younger people often relates to issues not relevant to the aged — fear of pregnancy and deep emotional involvement. The benefits of sex for the aged in nursing homes would derive from the motivation to care for themselves, and to be more alert and attractive.

A further issue concerns the responsibility of the nursing home toward the confused ill aged. The intellectually or psychiatrically impaired residents present the major problems associated with sex in the institution. In my experience in the nursing home field, the fact that the intellectually impaired have lost impulse control in a social situation places great responsibility on the nursing home to make certain that these patients behave in the way they would have wished to behave when they were well.

Implications regarding sex and the ill aged in nursing homes are far-reaching, affecting patients, families, staff, board members, volunteers, visiting professionals, and the community. Governmental fiats notwithstanding, important questions remain unanswered. Sexual behavior of the intact aged presents significant administrative problems. Sexual behavior of the impaired and the resulting sequelae present moral dilemmas worthy of microscopic analysis. Government has intruded into an area where angels should fear to tread! Since angels have better sense, government has no place in this area of social and personal behavior.

References

Berezin, M. Romance and the aged. *Time,* June 4, 1973.

de Beauvoir, S. *The coming of age.* New York: G. P. Putnam, 1972.

Comfort, A. The next patient right: Sex in the nursing home. *Modern Healthcare,* June 1974, p. 56.

Federal Register. Skilled Nursing Facilities. Washington: Department of Health, Education & Welfare, *39* (193), Part 2, October 3, 1974.

Freeman, J. J. Sexual capacity in the aging male. *Geriatrics,* 1961, 16, 37-43.

Kinsey, A. C., Pomeroy, W. B., & Martin, C. F. *Sexual behavior in the human male.* Philadelphia: W. B. Saunders, 1948.

Lobsenz, N. M. Sex and the senior citizen. *New York Times Magazine,* January 20, 1974.

Mace, D. R. The sexual, marital, and familial needs of the aging. Position paper on behalf of the National Council on Family Relations to the White House Conference on Aging, 1971.

Newman, G., & Nichols, C. R. Sexual activities and attitudes in older persons. *Journal of the American Medical Association,* 1960, *173,* 33-35.

Pfeiffer, E. Sexual behavior in old age. In E. W. Busse & E. Pfeiffer (Eds.), *Behavior and adaptation in later life.* Boston: Little, Brown, 1968.

Footnotes

[1] Reprinted, with permission, from Volume III, Number 3 (Summer, 1975) of the Journal of Long-Term Care Administration, published by the American College of Nursing Home Administrators.

The Second Language of Sex[1]

13

Robert N. Butler and Myrna I. Lewis

Can sex really remain interesting and exciting after forty, fifty or sixty years of adulthood? Older people themselves have testified that it can. Affection, warmth, and sensuality do not have to deteriorate with age and may, in fact, increase.

Sex in later life is sex for its own sake: pleasure, release, communication, shared intimacy. Except for older men married to younger women, it is no longer associated with childbearing and the creation of families. This freedom can be both exhilarating and insightful, especially for those who have literally never had the time until now to think about and get to know themselves and each other.

Love and sex can mean many different things to older people. Some of them will be obvious to you; others less so:

The opportunity for expression of passion, affection, admiration, loyalty and other positive emotions. This can occur in long-term relationships which have steadily grown and developed over the years, in relationships which actually improve in later years, and in new relationships such as second marriages.

176

An affirmation of one's body and its functioning. Active sex demonstrates to older persons that their bodies are still capable of working well and providing pleasure. For many people, satisfactory sexual functioning is an extremely important part of their lives and helps to maintain high morale and enthusiasm.

A strong sense of self. Sexuality is one of the ways people get a sense of their identity – who they are and their impact on others. Positive reactions from others preserve and enhance self-esteem. Feeling "feminine" or "masculine" is connected with feeling valued as a person. "I am now old" is quite different from feeling "I am older, and I can still see that others find me sexually appealing." Negative reactions depress and discourage older people and may tempt them to write off their sexuality forever.

A means of self-assertion. The patterns of self-assertion available when people are young change as they grow older. Their children are grown-up and gone, their jobs are usually behind them. Personal and social relationships now become far more important as outlets for expressing personality. Sex can be a valuable means of positive self-assertion. One man told us, "I feel like a million dollars when I make love even though we are scrimping along on Social Security. My wife has always made me feel like a great success in bed and I believe I do the same for her. We've been able to stand a lot of stress in life because of our closeness this way."

Protection from anxiety. The intimacy and the closeness of sexual union bring security and significance to people's lives, particularly when the outside world threatens them with hazards and losses. An older couple we know described the warmth of their sexual life as "a port in the storm," a place to escape from worry and trouble. Another older woman, aware of eventual death, called sex "the ultimate closeness against the night." Sex serves as a very important means of feeling in charge at a time when other elements of one's life tend to get out of control more frequently.

Defiance of the stereotypes of aging. Familiar though they are with the derogatory attitudes of society toward late-life sex, older people who are sexually active defy the neutered status expected of them. We have had them say to us, "We're not finished yet," "I'm not ready to kick the bucket," "You can't keep a good man [woman] down," or "There may be snow on the roof but there's still fire in the furnace."

The pleasure of being touched or caressed. Older widows and widowers tell us how much they now miss the simple pleasure and warmth of physical closeness, of being touched, held and caressed by someone they care for. Holding and hugging friends, children and pets offers some compensation but does not replace the special intimacy and feeling of being cared about that can exist in a good relationship or sexual union.

A sense of romance. The courting aspects of sexuality may be highly significant — flowers, soft lights, music, a sense of romantic pursuit, elegance, sentiment and courtliness — and give pleasure in themselves. Romance may continue even when sexual intercourse, for various reasons, ceases. Mr. and Mrs. Denham, a couple in their eighties, described their evenings together to us. They typically bathe and dress for dinner, she in a long dress, he in a suit and tie. They dine with candlelight and music, and put the dishes aside until morning. They continue to listen to music from their record library during the evening, holding hands, chatting and enjoying each other's companionship. At bedtime they bid each other good night and fall asleep in each other's arms. Often they awaken in the middle of the night and have long, intimate conversations, sleeping late the next morning. Mr. Denham said of his wife, "I fall in love with her every day. My feelings grow stronger when I realize we have only a certain amount of time left."

An affirmation of life. Sex expresses joy and continued affirmation of life. The quality of one's most intimate relationships is an important measure of whether life has been worthwhile. An otherwise successful person may count his life a failure if he has been unable to achieve significant closeness to other persons because he has never felt fully desired or accepted. Conversely, people with modest accomplishments may feel highly satisfied about themselves if they have been affirmed through intimate relationships. Sex is only one way of achieving intimacy, of course, but it is an especially profound affirmation of the worthwhileness of life.

A continuing search for sensual growth and experience. Some older persons who find sex exciting and fascinating continue to search for ways to enhance it. Others are dissatisfied with their present sex lives and look for ways to improve them. Older people, as well as younger, seek marriage counseling, pursue divorces, remarry, or have affairs in the hope of finding what they are searching for. Many can find this growth and excitement within their present relationship.

Love and sex are twin arts requiring effort and knowledge. Only in fairy tales do people live happily ever after without working at it. It takes a continuous and active effort to master the processes which eradicate emotional distances between yourself and another. Responsibility toward another person as toward oneself is the golden rule of love. There is no motivation like truly caring for someone to encourage you to follow the rule. Add to this the knowledge, skills and time to cultivate a relationship, and love has a good chance of flourishing.

In studying older people Kinsey commented that those showing a decline in sexual interest seemed to be "affected by a psychological fatigue, a loss of interest in repetition of the same sort of experience, an exhaustion of the possibilities for exploring new techniques, new types of contacts, new situations." Apathy is epidemic among older persons in this country, not surprisingly, given the serious social, economic, health and personal problems so many of them must cope with. Drained and discouraged, many do elect to give up. But those who have continued to be, or have grown to become, lively and imaginative, despite their health, financial or other problems, are also numerous, and for them — as for you — personal relationships offer the richest of rewards.

When people are young and first getting used to sexuality, their sex tends to be urgent and explosive, involved largely with physical pleasure and in many cases the conception of children. This is the *first language of sex*. It is biological and instinctive, with wonderfully exciting and energizing potentialities. The process of discovering one's ability to be sexually desirable and sexually effective often becomes a way of asserting independence, strength, prowess, and power. The first language of sex has been much discussed and written about because it is easy to study and measure – one can tabulate physical response, frequency of contacts, forms of outlet, sexual positions, and physical skills in love-making. But sex is not just a matter of athletics and "production." Some young people recognize this early on and simultaneously develop a *second language of sex* which is emotional and communicative as well as physical. Others continue largely in the first language – sometimes all their lives, sometimes only until they begin to see its limitations and desire something more.

The second language is largely learned rather than instinctive, and is often vastly underdeveloped since it depends upon your ability to recognize and share feelings in words, actions, and unspoken perceptions, and to achieve a mutual tenderness and thoughtfulness between yourself and another person. In its richest form the second language becomes highly creative and imaginative, with bountiful possibilities for new emotional experiences. Yet it is a slow-developing art, acquired deliberately and painstakingly through years of experience in giving and receiving.

In the natural flow of events in the life cycle times will come when you may find yourself re-evaluating many areas of your life, including your sexuality. Middle age is the time when people typically begin to take stock of their lives and reassess their work, their personal relationships, their social and spiritual commitments. Retirement is another time when re-evaluations take place. Both periods can be chaotic, generating emotional upsets, divorce, higher risk of alcoholism, and other evidences of stress.

But these can be constructive as well as dangerous ages, and the second language of sex has a good deal to offer you if you want to move in new directions in your personal life. Shared tenderness, warmth, humor, merriment, anger, passion, sorrow, camaraderie, fear – feelings of every conceivable sort can flow back and forth in a sexual relationship which has matured to this level of development.

Part of the secret of learning the second language lies in learning how to give. Receiving is much easier. It makes few demands. But the habit of only taking deadens the impulse to reciprocate. As Erich Fromm has said, "Most people see the problem of love primarily as that of being loved, rather than that of loving, of one's capacity to love." Giving is *not* an endless gift of yourself to others in which you expect nothing in return. Nor is it a marketplace transaction, trading with the expectation of an equal exchange. Healthy giving involves not only the hopeful and human anticipation that something equally good will be returned but also the pleasures inherent in giving, regardless of return. The balance to be struck must be chosen by each person and worked out in partnership.

The second language implies sensitivity. It means clearing up long-held grudges and old irritations toward your partner and people in general so your energy is not wasted in negativity. It suggests the possibility of renewing love every day. It requires knowing what pleases your partner and what pleases you. It involves playfulness as well as passion, and talking, laughing, teasing, sharing secrets, reminiscing, telling jokes, making plans, confessing fears and uncertainties, crying – in and out of the warmth of bed, in privacy and companionship. It need not always involve the sex act at all.

If boredom creeps into the relationship, both partners need to acknowledge it; it is time to look for or listen to the deeper feelings that each of you has hidden away against the time when the richness of such feelings will be welcome and restorative. You have to resist *actively* the pulls of habit. Routines and responsibilities may have dulled the impulse to really talk, and you must fight against succumbing to the temptation to withdraw into your own individual world. Self-centeredness, and wanting sexual and emotional contact only when you are in the mood without concern for your partner's needs, is guaranteed to produce conflict. Competitiveness based on some fancied level of sexual performance is also deadly.

The second language of sex can be developed by *anyone willing to try*. Every day in our professional practice we see older people who have struggled courageously throughout their lives to overcome obstacles, to earn a living, raise a family, and carry out other responsibilities. In so doing they have literally sacrificed their private lives and individual growth to this process. No matter. Love and sex are *always* there to be rediscovered, enhanced or even appreciated for the very first time, whether you are young or very old. Self-starters have the advantage over those who wait passively for love to strike like lightning.

Older people have, in fact, a special ability to bring love and sex to new levels of development literally because they are older. They develop perceptions which are connected with the unique sense of having lived a long time and having struggled to come to terms with life as a cycle from birth to death. A number of these qualities are beautifully suited to the flourishing of the second language. An appreciation of the preciousness of life and the valuing of immediateness can occur as people become older. What counts now is the present moment, where once it was the casually expected future. If the growing awareness of the brevity of life leads you to come to terms with your own mortality in a mature and healthy way, no longer denying it, you will find you no longer live heedlessly, as though you had all the time in the world. The challenge of living as richly as possible in the time you have left is exhilarating, not depressing.

Elementality — the enjoyment of the elemental things of life — may develop in late life precisely because older people are more keenly aware that life is short. They tell us that they find themselves becoming adept in separating out the important from the trivial. Responsiveness to nature, human contact, children, music, to beauty in any form, may be heightened. Healthy late life is frequently a time for greater enjoyment of all the senses — colors, sights, sounds, smells, touch — and less involvement with the transient drives for achievement, possessions, and power.

Older people have time for love. Although they have fewer years left to live than the young and middle-aged, if they are in reasonably good health, they can often spend more time on social and sexual relationships than any other age group. It is true that many have limited financial resources, but fortunately social and personal relationships are among the pleasures in life which can be free of charge.

Experience counts too. Many people *do* learn from experience. It is possible to become quite different in later life from what you were in youth. Obviously, the change can go in positive or negative directions. But the thing to remember is that change is possible. You do not need to become locked into any particular mode of behavior at any time of life. Experimentation and learning are possible all along the life cycle, and this holds true for sex and love. Naturally, the more actively you grow, the greater the reservoir of experience and the larger the repertoire you can draw upon in getting along with and loving other people. A man in his seventies gave this description of the bond between himself and his wife after forty-four years of marriage. "Sometimes I look at her in the morning and she does the same thing to me. We don't say anything, not even 'Good morning.' We understand each other. She is in bed when I get up and she'll look up and there are lots of things we don't have to say. 'You love me and I love you.' We have been married a long time and I think we understand each other."

Perhaps only in the later years can life with its various possibilities have the chance to shape itself into something approximating a human work of art. And perhaps only in later life, when personality reaches its final stages of development, can love-making and sex achieve the fullest possible growth. Sex does not merely exist after sixty; it holds the possibility of becoming greater than it ever was. It can be joyful and creative, healthy and health-giving. It unites human beings in an affirmation of love, and is therefore also morally right and virtuous. Those older persons who have no partners and must experience sex alone need to know that this, too, is their right — a healthy giving to oneself that reflects a strong sense of self-esteem and worth. Those who informed us as we wrote this book have given every one of us a valuable gift — a realistic expectation of sex after sixty.

Footnotes

[1] "The Second Language of Sex" (pp. 136-145) from *Sex After Sixty* by Robert N. Butler, M.D. and Myrna I. Lewis. Copyright ©1976 by Robert N. Butler, M.D. and Myrna I. Lewis. Reprinted by permission of Harper & Row, Publishers, Inc.

What Happens to Love? Love, Sexuality and Aging

14

Margaret Neiswender Reedy

"We have come closer, more content with each other
in these 46 years. We continue to be thrilled with
each other's presence and that sense of attraction that
began the first time we met is the same now — only a
thousand times deeper and tenderer."[1]

Our need for love and human intimacy is lifelong. How
well love born in youth can weather the years is a serious
concern for many people. Our uncertainties about the nature
of love in later life are reflected in the jokes we tell. Many
jokes imply that there can be love and attraction, but not sex
in the later years. For example, "At your age, there's a lot of
will, but no way." Other jokes suggest that love is somehow
no longer love at all: "Definition of old age: When you know
you love your wife, but can't remember why." All joking
aside, what happens to love in the later years?

The purpose of this paper is to describe the nature of
love and its relationship to sexual intimacy in satisfying love
relationships between older men and women. To understand
what happens to love, five questions need to be answered.

First, what is love? Second, how satisfying are love relationships between older men and women? Third, what are satisfying love relationships like in later life? Fourth, in what ways does love change as lovers grow older together? Finally, what happens to sexual intimacy?

What Is Love, Anyway?

Long ago Elizabeth Barrett Browning said it well when she wrote, "How do I love thee? Let me count the ways." There is little agreement on exactly what love is. For most, including philosophers and social scientists, love is easier to fall into or out of than to define. As other papers in this collection point out, people are sexual beings and seek human contact and warmth throughout their lives. Clearly, the pleasure of sexual intimacy and the comfort of physical contact is one way of expressing love. Although sexuality is an important and essential dimension of love, there is more to love than sex.

---

[1] Much of the material presented in this chapter is abstracted from a broader study of the characteristics of satisfying love relationships between men and women from young adulthood to later maturity. Among the participants in the study were 34 older couples who ranged in age from 58 to 84 years, with an average age of 65. On the average, these couples had been married 37 years and had raised two children. Nearly all had finished high school and some college, although this was less characteristic of the women. Those who were currently working, as well as those who were retired, were typically in professional occupations or in skilled technical or clerical work. About one-third of the older women were homemakers.

Each couple was nominated to participate in the study by a person who knew the couple well and who judged them to have an especially satisfying love relationship. Participants wrote answers to questions about what made their relationship satisfying and how their relationship had changed over time. Each person also described his or her current love relationship by indicating that each of a series of statements described the relationship very well, somewhat, or not at all. These statements had been previously classified by judges into six categories reflecting six different dimensions of loving: (1) emotional security, (2) respect, (3) helping and playing behaviors, (4) communication, (5) loyalty, and (6) sexual intimacy. Looking at the way individuals rated the statements, we could understand which of the six dimensions of loving were most important to love and which were least important.

A close look at the conceptions of love offered in the historical and research literature on love suggests that there are six dimensions of loving: emotional security, respect, helping and playing behaviors, communication, loyalty, and sexual intimacy. Let's look at each of these six dimensions. First, there is emotional security. Emotional security refers to feelings of trust, caring, concern, and closeness in the relationship. Lovers who feel emotionally secure in their relationship really feel that they can count on one another. Another dimension of love is respect. Since disagreement and conflict between lovers is inevitable, respect in love means being able to be tolerant, understanding, and patient. Lovers who respect each other can accept the fact that their partner does not always share the same interests. When there is respect in love, an individual is likely to agree that "my partner makes good decisions," and that "I am confident that he (or she) can succeed at whatever he (or she) wants to do."

A third aspect of love is that lovers enjoy spending time together, working as well as playing. Partners are willing to help each other out and to make sacrifices for each other. Common interests and shared life goals as well as sharing activities and experiences strengthen the bond of love between two people. The fourth dimension of love is communication. Communication in love means being able to be honest and self-revealing. Lovers who value communication in their relationship can confide in each other, can talk about feelings of uncertainty and sadness as well as happiness, and can be good listeners.

Loyalty is the fifth dimension of love. Loyalty involves a sense of investment in and a commitment to the future of the relationship. Lovers who are loyal are likely to believe that "The future is sure to be beautiful as long as we are together." Finally, sexual intimacy is an important dimension of love. Sexual intimacy involves sexual attraction, passionate desire, and pleasurable love making as well as feelings of tenderness, affection, and warmth. In expressing sexual intimacy, lovers want to give sexual pleasure to one another and enjoy making love.

Although I am sure that you can think of couples you know who emphasize one way of loving while other couples emphasize another, these are all important dimensions of love. In the following sections, we will see how important these different aspects of loving are from youth to later maturity.

Love After Parenthood: A Second Honeymoon

Historically, the post-parental period of married life is new. At the turn of the century, it was rare for both partners to live to see their last child marry and leave home. Today, because people are living longer, having smaller families, and finishing childrearing sooner, marital partners can expect to share a life together for ten or twenty years after their children leave home. Today, men are about 54 and women are about 51 when their last child is married (Norton, 1974).

It appears that parenthood is hard on love relationships. Being a mother or a father makes it harder for an individual to feel good about being a lover, a partner in marriage, a husband, or a wife. To be happy in love is easiest when a couple is married without children, or when a couple is older and finished with the child-rearing business. Studies of marital satisfaction in the adult years (Rollins and Feldman, 1970; Troll, 1971; Campbell, 1975) show that satisfaction with marriage is at its highest for newlyweds. Almost as soon as a couple has children, the happy honeymoon is over. After children are born, men and women (but especially women) report less satisfaction and happiness with their relationship. Boyd Rollins and Harold Feldman (1970), in a study of over 800 married couples, found that marital satisfaction decreases during the early adult years of childbearing, and reaches a low point just before teenage sons and daughters leave home for good. Couples in mid-life generally report less communication, companionship, and affection compared to the earliest years of marriage.

If couples can wait until their children leave home, they are quite likely to experience a kind of "second honeymoon." In their study, Boyd Rollins and Harold Feldman (1970) reported that couples with an "empty nest" were as satisfied with their marriage as the newly-married couples without children. Once the children are gone, couples find they have more time for each other and partners can get to know each other again. As one older woman, married 42 years, said, "After the children are gone, there is more time to do things together alone. We spent years of doing things with our children. After they were gone, we found out how nice it is to be alone. If couples can get through the first part, the rest of life can be great."

Other couples note that once children are grown and gone, there are fewer responsibilities, leading to a new sense of freedom. One woman who had raised five children describes the changes in her love relationship this way, "It's grown and ripened like vintage wine. The bouquet, color, and heady flavor were always there, but now, being free of the responsibility of child-rearing, we've more delight in one another than ever. We haven't lived charmed lives. We've had the normal allotment of ups and downs and a three-year separation during the war, but we've always felt secure in our marriage."

Most post-parental couples find that being alone together is a great pleasure. In terms of its effect on satisfaction with love and marriage, raising a family appears to be something that is less than fun to do and more fun to have done.

Happy Love Relationships in Later Life: What Are They Like?

What are the characteristics of satisfying love relationships between older men and women? What is most valued between married lovers in later life? When we looked at the way older men and women described their relationships, we found that, as a group, older lovers valued emotional security most in their love relationships. For older lovers, being able to depend on one another as well as being able to trust one another were central to love. One 68 year old woman, who had recently taken up modern dancing, described it this way, "There is great comfort in knowing he is there to help me when I need help." What makes the relationship satisfying for another man is that "She demonstrates love and caring by word and deed. She helps me in protecting my health, appearance, and comfort. She conserves our resources, giving me a feeling of security." For these couples, security does not mean being *dependent*. Rather, it means being able to *depend on* each other.

In addition to feeling secure in love, it is important to be respected and admired. Respect was rated the second most important aspect of love for older lovers. One 60 year old man explained what makes his relationship satisfying for him this way: "She always understands my needs and allows me to seek goals I have for myself in addition to sharing in goals we have for our family. She allows me to have my up and down moods and respects my need to sometimes be by myself. I have no doubts of her love for me, which is very comforting." Respect for some older couples means being able to be good friends as well as lovers.

The third most important dimension of love was the ability to communicate and be honest with each other. For one past military man, being "able to share in everything — with no secrets — and being willing to confide in each other" made the relationship satisfying for him. A 62 year old insurance salesman put it this way: "I share my joys, sorrows, and adventures with her and she does the same with me, giving us twice as much fun as we would have individually."

The fourth most important dimension of love was spending time together working and playing. One 84 year old woman, married 62 years, focused on the mutual effort to work together in life, "I've tried to make our home a place of love and happiness. I wanted him to look forward to coming home. I wanted to pull my share. Being able to manage within our budget has been important." A 64 year old banker also emphasized the pleasure of building a life together, "There is a lot to do — emotional, financial, creative, routine — in establishing a home, becoming a family, raising and educating children. I feel each of us has put in a full-time share — it has been a shared enterprise, and both the sharing and the enterprise have given me deep and broad satisfaction." Another 59 year old woman, returning to college for a master's degree, takes pleasure in the time spent together, "We like to do things together. We always have, but it's even more fun now since we don't get to do many things alone. For example, one weekend all the kids happened to be gone and we had a blast just being home alone together."

Sexual intimacy was the fifth most important dimension of love. This does not mean that sex is unimportant to love in later life. One 60 year old expresses his satisfaction this way,

"She is physically pleasing to all my senses — different at different times of life, but always pleasing." An intensive care nurse described what makes her love relationship satisfying for her in this way: "I cherish his ability to be tender. He responds to my sexual needs. Most of our sexual activity is a mutual passionate expression of feeling close together. But each of us responds to the other's sexual advance when either might not be quite ready."

Finally, loyalty was the least emphasized dimension of love. Although commitment to each other and to the future was important, it was just less important compared to the other aspects of loving. Also, some older lovers valued loyalty and faithfulness more than others. For one older mother of three, what makes her relationship satisfying is that "He is steadfast and true and acts as though he expects to spend the rest of his life with me." And for another, "We have always been aware that the intensity of our feelings has an ebb and flow, and we have floated on the low tides, certain that the high tides would soon and always return."

One question immediately comes to mind. Are these the same characteristics that are important to satisfaction in love relationships in young adulthood and in mid-life? Based on our findings, the answer to this question appears to be both "yes" and "no." First, let's look at the "yes" part of the answer. We found that young and middle-aged adults rank the six dimensions of loving in *exactly* the same order of importance as older adults do, with emotional security at the top of the list. This tells us that at any age the feeling that "I can trust him" or "I really care for her" are most central to love, followed by the ability to be respectful, accepting, and tolerant in love. We also found that at any age there is more to love than sex. From youth to later maturity, sexual intimacy was rated as the fifth most important dimension of loving. In short, we found that the valued aspects of love relationships appear to be quite stable from one age period to the next.

We also found evidence for change in the nature of love with age. This is the "no" part of the answer to the question posed above. We found that, while all age groups rank the six dimensions of loving in the same order of importance, older men and women place even more value on emotional security compared to their younger counterparts. This suggests that, as lovers grow older, love becomes more of what it has always been – a source of security, warmth, comfort, and support. As one older man put it, "I don't believe our relationship has changed much except to grow deeper and more solid, with increased understanding and tolerance of each other. There have been periods of varying intensity, but the core of warmth and devotion was always present, sustaining, and satisfying."

The Mellowing of Love: When Lovers Grow Old Together

When we asked older men and women to describe how their love relationship had changed since they first met, a common theme was that their love was the same, yet different. Personal experience suggests that the nature of love changes with age as our needs change during development. For example, the needs of an infant and the nature of the love relationship between infant and mother are different from the needs and kind of love which blossoms when a man and a woman first meet. Similarly, the nature of a new love relationship between adults is going to be different from the bond that unites a man and a woman after 50 years of living and loving.

When describing the changes in their relationship over time, many older couples noted that their relationship has become closer and deeper. There is the sense that this change comes by having experienced the ebb and flow of life together, by having weathered the bad times and enjoyed the good times. One retired school teacher described the change in love this way, "Our love has deepened, our understanding of each other has grown. Our life experiences together have drawn us closer together." A greater sense of affection and understanding makes the relationship closer for some older lovers. One man described the changes in his 54 year old love relationship with a bit of "tongue in cheek": "It has changed from exciting, romantic thrills to comfortable, warm, happy affection. Our vigor has certainly lessened. Our problems are fewer and different. We have switched from making and caring for babies to caring for doctors, politicians, and tax collectors."

A second theme is that there is now more patience, acceptance, and tolerance for the partner after so many years together. When asked how their relationship might be changed to make it more satisfactory, one 70 year old career woman replied, "Any changes to be made after over 50 years of a satisfactory happily married life would be of a minor nature. Some traits or characteristics, with age, are not easily eliminated, but with mutual patience and understanding can be overlooked and lived with." Whereas young adults seem to struggle at accepting each other's weaknesses as well as strengths, satisfied older lovers seem to really be able to accept one another.

Altogether, there is a sense that the relationship has mellowed. One 71 year old former cabinetmaker described 48 years of married life in one succinct sentence, "Growing old together mellows the partners in many ways." Changes in the nature of sexual intimacy contribute to this sense of mellowness and ripening of love. One man who was starting a second career wrote about his 40 year marriage, "Our relationship has improved with age. It has warmed and mellowed. At one time an important element of our relationship, although never the most important element, was the marvelous sexual satisfaction that we enjoyed with considerable frequency. As we have grown older, this aspect has assumed less importance, to be replaced to some extent by less exciting manifestations of our love and affection such as frequent touching, holding, hugging, kissing, and, of course, continual verbal expressions of love. We feel that at this time we are as much in love, if not more so, than we ever were, as we have a chance to thoroughly enjoy each other exclusively now that our children are grown and have 'left the fold.'" For many, there is more tenderness, affection, and warmth. The nature of love is different, yet equally satisfying.

New Dimensions in Sexual Intimacy: Cuddling and Closeness

When older men and women describe their relationships, many emphasize that continuing physical and sexual attraction for one another is central to their relationship. When asked to describe the characteristics of the relationship that have been important in making it last, one former executive of a large corporation said, "A strong sex drive, a physical and emotional attraction which, at least for me, is profoundly satisfied and constantly reawakened." For some, there is a continuing delight and sense of awe about the relationship: "After forty years, I am still mystified about 'Why me?' I try to make known to him my continued delight in our love. He has always been attractive to me physically. I respond with pleasure in our sexual relations."

Still, the nature of sexuality and sexual intimacy in the later years has a different quality. Older couples report that sexual intercourse is less frequent, but that it is as pleasurable as in youth. A grandmother for the first time at 62, one woman notes that, "Although the sexual aspects are not as demanding as in earlier years, it is still a happy experience." There is also a new dimension to sexual love in the later years. More than the act of intercourse, sexual intimacy between older lovers means tenderness, a gentle touch, an affectionate embrace, and just the other's physical presence. As one 70 year old woman, married 42 years, put it: "In the beginning there was a great sexual love and respect for each other. Years later, we make love less often but we have a lot of affection for each other. It is important to cuddle when you are older." And another woman, "At this time, it is infinitely comforting to cuddle up to him when I am lonely during the night." The youthful fires of passion are quieter now. Different and more subtle evidence of affection becomes important. Giving his wife a hug, one 75 year old man said, "I show her that I love her and need her with candy, cards, and flowers. I also hug and kiss her often." A smile, a nod of the head, a wink, a kiss, a hug, cuddling, and physical closeness take on added meaning in sexual expressions of love between older lovers. In addition to the immediate pleasure of physical intimacy, sexuality becomes an affirmation of a lifetime of shared experiences and memories.

What Makes Relationships Last?
The Importance of Expectations

Contrary to the "happy ever after" fairy tale, satisfying love relationships are not simply "dreams come true" — at least not without effort. As one woman put it, "The key to a

successful marriage is to *make it work."* Making a relationship last means caring about it enough to be patient, to listen,
and to talk through the difficult times.

It is interesting that many older men and women claim
that their commitment to a lifelong relationship is an
important reason why their relationship has endured over the
years. As one 67 year old former actor said, "In the first
place, we wanted it to last. I found a girl I admired and
respected and loved; really hot love! We talked over what we
wanted, liked, and disliked, and agreed on the objectives. We
helped each other to grow, both together and separately. I
believe that because of our conscious effort to be tolerant,
loving, and open to learn we have overcome many obstacles
and problems." The idea is that love, like sexual activity, is
lifelong if you believe it is.

Beyond the expectation that the relationship will last,
older lovers believe that mutual admiration, respect, and
caring, trust and security, similar basic value systems, and
physical attraction are central elements in a lasting relationship. Finally, the ability to talk openly with each other, to
express likes and dislikes, and to enjoy one another's
company and companionship make a lasting relationship
possible. One man said it this way, "I would rather be with
her than with anyone."

What I hope I've shown you is that the nature of love
and sexual intimacy between older lovers has less to do with
intense excitement and more to do with tenderness,
affection, understanding, touching, warmth, and physical
closeness. Love and sexuality in the later years are an
affirmation of present aliveness and past shared experiences.
Reflecting on his 40 year old love relationship, one man tells
what can happen to love: "We have had four children whose
growth, companionship, and love was and is greatly
enriching. We have lived a life from youth to age, rarely
apart, always preferring to be together. We have always
known an intense joy in each other and in our children. It
was lovely when it began; it still is. I do not think it has
changed for better or worse; it has only grown stronger and
deeper, accumulated a richness of shared living and loving,
shared problems and happiness. It's been the best. It still is.
What more can I say?"

References

Campbell, A. The American way of mating. *Psychology Today,* May 1975, pp. 37-40; 42-43.

Norton, A. J. The family life cycle updated: Components and uses. In R. F. Winch & G. B. Spanier (Eds.), *Selected Studies in marriage and the family.* New York: Holt, Rinehart, & Winston, 1974.

Reedy, M. N. Age and sex differences in personal needs and the nature of love: A study of happily married young, middle-aged, and older adult couples. Unpublished doctoral dissertation, University of Southern California, 1977.

Rollins, B., & Feldman, H. Marital satisfaction through the life span. *Journal of Marriage and the Family,* 1970, *32,* 20-27.

Troll, L. E. The family of later life: A decade review. *Journal of Marriage and the Family,* 1971, *33,* 263-290.